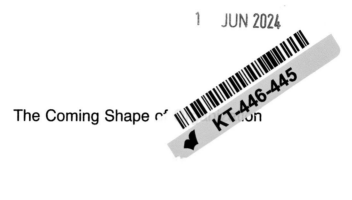

The Coming Shape of ... ...on

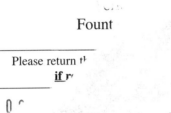

Fount

Please return t'
if r'

0 ʿ

By the same author

How to Build a Successful Team ... the Belbin Way (CD-ROM)

The Job Promoters

Management Teams: Why They Succeed or Fail

Team Roles At Work

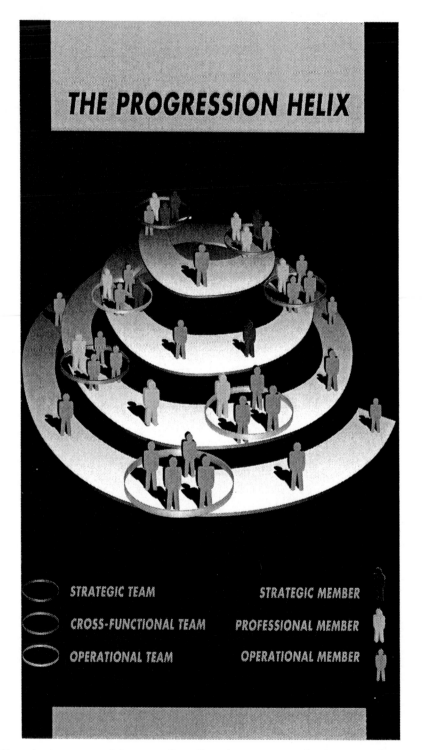

Organizations are evolving away from formal structures in the direction of processes.
The progression helix depicts one favoured model (see also page 111).

The Coming Shape of Organization

Meredith Belbin

Butterworth-Heinemann
Linacre House, Jordan Hill, Oxford OX2 8DP
225 Wildwood Avenue, Woburn, MA 01801-2041
A division of Reed Educational & Professional Publishing Ltd

$\mathcal{R}$ A member of the Reed Elsevier plc group

OXFORD   AUCKLAND   BOSTON
JOHANNESBURG   MELBOURNE   NEW DELHI

First published 1996
Reprinted 1996
Paperback edition 1998
Reprinted 1999

British Library Cataloguing in Publication Data
Belbin, R. M.
    The Coming Shape of Organization
    I. Title
    658.402

ISBN 0 7506 3950 4

Transferred to digital printing 2005

Composition by Genesis Typesetting, Laser Quay, Rochester, Kent

Contents ────────────────

Prologue   vi

Acknowledgements   xi

  1 In search of the future   1
  2 The faltering organization   8
  3 The problem with Mr Big   14
  4 Lessons from a diminutive masterclass   23
  5 Concurrent versus sequential decision-making   33
  6 Replacing traditional hierarchy   41
  7 An alternative way of arranging work   48
  8 Teams communicate with teams   56
  9 Employing the highly talented   64
10 The culture and the organization   70
11 Strategic leadership comes of age   77
12 The organization of public affairs   84
13 Forces making for change   96
14 The evolution of common shape   104

Epilogue   116

Appendix 1: Exercises   119

Appendix 2: The nine team roles   122

Further reading   123

Index   125

Prologue

Whereas the past or the present have occupied the focus of most of my previous writings, this book is focused on the future. This is a subject on which it is not possible to write as authoritatively as on events that have already taken place. While I want to avoid the risk of slipping into speculations that can be neither proved nor disproved, I believe that the seeds of the future have been set down in the past, are contained in the present and can be detected through careful analysis of the contemporary scene. This chosen method of approach will be elaborated in Chapter 1.

The importance of the subject, however, cannot be questioned. Perspectives on the future underlie all our efforts. We cannot steer even in the short-term without having some sense of the direction in which we are travelling.

The particular aspect of the future which this book discusses is the nature and effectiveness of organizations. These vehicles for human endeavour are driven by managers and it is to them and to students of Management that this book is addressed. I will begin with a message: organizations should not be taken for granted. They are capable of change, or rather of being changed, for it certainly will not happen without purposive intervention. But the time is now ripe for that change to take place. Hierarchy is an approach to Organization that is beginning to lose its once unquestioned authority where it exists in its more extreme form; in multilevel hierarchy, which gives rise to multilevel bureaucracy, and absolute hierarchy, where all work is determined by downward assignment and where peers play no part in distributing work among themselves. History has imposed these forms of organization upon us. They will be displaced only if we find something better.

As it happened, serendipity played its due part in placing Organization on the current agenda of industry. Something unexpectedly valuable was learned from the last recession. Firms were obliged to make cut-backs at every level. Delayering was simply one of a number of ways of putting economy measures into effect. Then, to the surprise of many, this modified organization was found to function more efficiently and it became easier to get things done. Many management pundits were put on the defensive by this discovery. After all, if better results stemmed from changes taken under pressure, why had those improvements not been foreseen as desirable during normal times?

Organization is about how people relate to one another when engaged in joint endeavours. The subject first claimed my attention when I ventured outside the academic world into the realms of industry. My immediate assignment was to improve productivity and quality. After an association with experienced management consultants, I discovered a more effective way of achieving the same goal: it lay in finding the most suitable people to carry particular responsibilities. From that moment on I became closely involved in personnel selection. The experience gained in the assessment of individual talents, along with the professional tools that we developed to meet the need, opened the opportunity for myself and my colleagues to conduct research at Henley Management College. Interest had there developed in teamwork and in particular the College wanted to know why some teams of individually able executives performed poorly and others well.

The results of that research were published in my book *Management Teams: Why They Succeed or Fail*. In short, we discovered that it was the combination of particular individuals rather than the merits of individuals themselves that accounted for what was achieved: success or failure could be predicted, within certain limits. Later we devised new ways of improving team selection and performance. The outcome was Interplace, a computer-based human resource management system now used in many parts of the world.

At this point it might be supposed I had reached journey's end. If companies recruit the right people and assemble them in the most balanced and well designed teams with the aid of an expert system, the desired results should follow. Firms which took that approach should thrive.

But now I ran into a new phenomenon amid the peaks of boom and the troughs of depression that buffeted almost all companies operating in world competitive markets. Some companies weathered the storms and ploughed their way forward through the tumultuous waves that economic stresses generate. Others shipped water and were in danger of sinking. The surprise was that some companies, renowned for their management practices and reputed leadership, foundered while other supposedly lesser companies forged ahead.

My inquiries eventually led me to the view that the essential difference between the successful and unsuccessful companies lay in the quality of their decision-making. Yet good decision-making within an organization is a more complex business than is generally imagined. The fallacy, to which I had proved myself as susceptible as anyone else, was to assume that the recruitment and retention of able people in the aggregate, operating in well-balanced teams, would ensure better performance on the part of the organization as a whole. Broadly that is what tends to happen. Unfortunately, without taking a holistic view of the enterprise, nothing can be guaranteed. Even when all the requisite human resources are available, it does not necessarily ensure they are used in the right way.

The emerging truth is that the way things commonly stand, the overall effectiveness of a corporation depends largely on the decisions made by its head and not on the array of talents and potential talents that a corporation possesses. The effective utilization of the abilities available to an organization depends on how it is structured and led and on its basic dynamism. During the height of the recession it became apparent that some small businesses with a limited supply of able executives were conspicuously outperforming larger competitors who had hoarded a supply of top talents.

My explanation of the success of these up-and-coming companies was that they had found better ways of using human resources. Fewer people can outperform the many if they are put together in the right way. The construction of small, effective teams had become my special interest and the similarities began to grow between what we had found out in our experimental work in industry and what I was observing in industry.

But at the same time it transpired that the door had opened on to a bigger world. No less important than the team was the link between the team and the structure of the company. Even a good team cannot fulfil itself in an unsatisfactory environment. That is what led me to think about the design of Organization and which resulted in lecturing invitations in various parts of the country. The opportunity to put some of the ideas being formulated into practice soon followed. From that moment onwards I believe that my understanding of the subject moved forward at an accelerating pace.

On that count, and before commencing my exposition, I feel the need to make certain disclaimers. In the first place I have not attempted to make an academic evaluation of Organization; this I will leave to those who may be better qualified. Secondly, books that deal with comparisons in management practice usually cite particular companies in order to make the points both more valid and more vivid. This is a precedent I can scarcely follow. It would hardly be right for me to parade intimate information gained in confidential situations or to compromise my professional position. I have chosen therefore to write at a level of generality. That will not in any way deflect my intention of keeping as close as possible to observed realities.

The overall purpose of this book is to lay before the reader an exposition of how faulty organizational design has led to recurring problems in the world today and to indicate both the reasons why these designs are likely to be superseded and the form they will take. I believe the forces of evolution will play a great part in this process, as they have in the past, and I will contend that the most striking lessons that emerge can be extracted from the organizational accomplishments of the higher insects.

It is surprising how restricted one becomes in writing about Organization and its forms. There have in the past been so few varieties and models from which to choose that the very word has been hijacked for a wider usage: Organization commonly refers to any body to which employees belong and for which a synonym might be the firm, the company or the Council. In writing about Organization, where it is used as a construct about systems and in order to avoid competing meanings, I will crown the word with a capital letter O to avoid possible ambiguities. That honour, perhaps, will serve to give this important but neglected subject the renewed lease of life that it deserves!

Meredith Belbin

Acknowledgements

I am grateful to the many who have contributed information and observations included in this book and to my family on other counts; to my wife, Eunice, for picking up the errors and the gaps in the line of argument; to my son, Nigel, for taking over all duties in the office so that I could get on with the writing: and to my brother-in-law, Michael Kremer, for discriminating help throughout.

During my student days at Cambridge I played in the same rugby team and rowed in the same boat as David Attenborough, the long-term benefit of which has been the references he kindly supplied on the higher termites and his subsequent advice on the script; all of which has been greatly appreciated.

Earlier drafts of this book have been read by my colleagues in Australia, Dr David Marriott and John Burns, by Dr Len Goodstein in the USA, by Alan Marsden in Hong Kong and by Kathryn Grant of Butterworth-Heinemann in the UK; all have made helpful suggestions but are in no way responsible for the book's shortcomings.

1

In search of the future ─────────

It is a feature of the world today that people who are widely separated in space may still find themselves caught up in the same time capsule. This raises the question of where we stand in relation to time and whether we are managing time or time is managing us.

For a number of years I travelled at regular intervals between England and Australia, two countries positioned at opposite sides of the world and even for a period in a political sense also. Yet what surprised me in Australia corresponded more or less exactly with what surprised Australians in England, which was the remarkable similarity of their domestic scenes. In spite of its election of a Labor Government and its widely canvassed campaign to repudiate its traditional allegiance to the Queen and to declare itself a Republic, Australia had readily adopted Thatcherism and all that it implied from Britain. Its economic strategy was based on monetarism and the privatization of many functions previously belonging to the public sector. A belief in tight money had led to a reduction in the Public Sector Borrowing Requirement and an increase in interest rates. Both countries then shared the same socio-economic experiences: a reduced rate of inflation and a stronger currency, accompanied by a fall in property prices, a steep rise in unemployment and an increase in the crime rate.

Policies and programmes are now being transmitted across the world, copied and introduced with remarkable speed in a way that is comparable with the flow of international trade. Countries both export and import ideas. So, in a reciprocal fashion, while Britain exported to many parts of the world what was called Thatcherism, it became receptive itself to other introductions. Over an extended period the employment services had been de-professionalized as an economy measure with less skilled staff taking over what was left; but, to compensate, self-help Job Clubs were introduced from the United States as a means of providing low-cost help to the unemployed.

Radical policy changes in the public sector can soon override long accumulated national experience. Sweden, which had at one time been a major world player and standard-setter in developing policies to combat unemployment, abandoned many of those policies in the face of rising public debt. Taking on programmes in line with those operating in other developed countries, Sweden experienced the severest upturn in unemployment, especially youth unemployment, in over half a century. Most remarkable of all these revolutions has been the U-turn in the employment and economic policies of Communist China. Setting aside its previous inward-looking isolation, China's market liberalism has surpassed that of many avowed capitalist countries.

That the past is merging with the future at an amazing rate is also becoming evident to the many people who travel the world as tourists and who are not in the least theoretically minded. Modernity establishes itself cheek by jowl with the primitive and the traditional in developing countries: the bullock cart stands outside the high-rise block with its fast-moving elevators; laptop computers will be on sale next to the shop where all calculations are assisted by abacus.

Yet the rapid movement of policies and material goods should not be taken as the most significant pointer of the direction in which the world is going. What matters even more is the ultimate outcome between competing schools of thought in the world on how the future should be regarded and therefore approached.

From the passive to the proactive

Throughout much of human history the basic assumptions about the future were founded on a universal belief in predestination. The signals about fate, over which mortals have no control, were implanted in the regularities of nature. There was a rational basis for taking heed of them. Astronomy served as a guide to the future by acting as a long-term weather forecast providing leads on when crops should be gathered, stored and sown. It is little wonder that astronomy, with its proven utility, should lead to its supernatural cousin, astrology, which was to have such a long-lasting influence on human affairs and still stirs up so much popular attention and interest today. Astrology was founded on a belief that the gods were in the heavens, residing in the stars themselves and exercising their arcane powers over mortals. Such a belief did not preclude the existence of other means of discovering the messages of destiny. Chiromancy, geomancy, divination through inspection of the entrails, the reading of tarot cards and of tea leaves all staked their claims to portend the future.

What binds together all these is an underlying attitude of passivity towards what lies ahead, where fate is the ultimate controller. What we are witnessing now is a movement in the opposite direction. In place of fatalism there is a swing to the belief that gifted humans can create and manage the future given the possession of the requisite powers. And because it has the mandate and is carrying the expectations of the electorate, government wants to be seen to lead in the exercise of this ambition.

Yet the real problem in adopting a more proactive approach to the future is the dearth of information and sound ideas upon which decisions can be made. Admittedly, there are people who can be consulted with advantage. A new generation of advisers has taken over from the old conveyors of mystique. The newcomers bear the title of futurologists and their tools of trade mainly comprise sophisticated methods for collecting data and examining trends. From an extrapolation of figures a picture can be drawn as to how the world might look in the years ahead. The rise of the world's population can be projected into the middle of the next century. The cutting down of the forests and jungles will have some long-term predictable consequences and its implications for mankind can be projected. Such an extrapolation of trends, if carried far enough forward, usually results in an alarming picture with many futurologists pointing their fingers towards a doomsday scenario.

Accurate forecasting is certainly elusive, for the future does not move forward in a straight line. Counterbalancing forces come into play. Explosions in the population of pests are met with a commensurate rise in predators; diseases give rise to antibodies and there are few cases of continuing unconstrained growth. The future retains an element of unpredictability because there are no single determining forces. Instead, the relative balance of factors and components are changing in a continuously evolving system.

To sum up, the predominant players who deal with the future fall into three main groups. There are the awe-inspired and the awe-seekers who believe that humans are at the mercy of predestination about which the signs can be read by the chosen few; there are the vigorous managers who believe that the future can be managed much like the forward plans of a company and all that is needed is an adequacy of resources and some decisiveness; and there are the technocrats who believe that aspects of the future can be forecast by the techniques of analytical dissection.

Yet there is another approach that should be considered by those who are in the business of long-term strategic planning.

Managing evolution

The one force that has moved the world forward, continuously and irrevocably, since life began on Earth has been evolution, with its mechanisms for creating diversity and selecting those organisms best fitted to survive. We should not have the arrogance – nor do we possess the power – to resist evolution. But if we understand its character we may recognize that a moment in history has at last arrived where we can help that process along in a favourable direction.

What creates this opportunity is that the focus of advantage as it affects humans has changed. Over a great span of time, size and stature, hands that could fashion tools and mouths and minds adapted to engaging in complex communication, all played their part in bringing about the dominance of our species. Now it seems this process of physical development has halted. Differences in biologically based fitness to survive as between individuals and races with different characteristics can be virtually ruled out under the softer conditions of the modern world. But another form of differential survival has long been with us and is still staking out its claims. It is the differential survival of social systems.

Throughout recorded history particular civilizations have risen only to fall. They have reached their zenith at one period and become subject to all-round decline at another. The history of civilization is the history of social systems as they grappled with the natural phenomena of the world around them and responded to the economic pressures and opportunities that interaction with other groups presented. Tribal groupings gave way to imperial kingdoms to be replaced by feudalism which in turn was overtaken by capitalism. Capitalism, in its purest form, has been under pressure for some decades to transform itself into some further condition that is at yet indistinct but will be explored later in this book. Each of these successive stages has recognizable features of social organization which set it apart from each preceding stage.

So, too, different producer systems have evolved as they have become more successful. Cottage industries have grown into small businesses, later overtaken by medium-sized businesses, large businesses and so on to multinationals and transnationals. These stages are commonly distinguished from one another in terms of size. But no less important is the difference in the underlying organizational principles by which they are run. So the question has to be posed: was it the growth in size that fostered the development of a new set of organizational principles, or did the discovery of a better organizational formula become the prime factor in bringing about this growth?

Evolution in the private sector

Whatever it is that drives change, and whether it is recognized or not, evolution takes on a particular pattern. Given free competition between different companies, those with the most effective organizations will be the survivors.

It is here that communications technology is vastly speeding up the process of the evolution of enterprises. Multinationals know no frontiers and few political complications restrict their freedom to set up systems and organizations with a particular character. What is adopted in one location may be taken up the next day in a distant continent in another hemisphere. A further force making for rapid change is the movement of personnel between companies. Managers who switch jobs take what they have learned with them and are often valued for what they can introduce.

In the business world the pressure to change and to evaluate effectiveness is greater than that operating on government programmes. The pressures arise because businesses are in a constant state of competition with other businesses both within a country and on an international scale. A competitive advantage will account for why one business succeeds and another fails, even if the reasons underlying any apparent success are imperfectly understood. Just as in Darwinian theory it is unnecessary for an organism to possess consciousness of its competitive advantage, for its mere possession is sufficient to overcome competitors, so also diversity in business practices leads to evolutionary progress.

The share values of a company may fluctuate on the stock exchange as a direct response to its past performance. But those who wish to get ahead of the market and have eyes on the future will be looking for signs that portend well for a company or which can be taken as warning signals. Here aspects of Organization are increasingly gaining attention. At one time the market was mainly attracted to the great captains of industry or the most famous entrepreneurs. Over time it was found that the shares of their companies would tend to be oversubscribed or overvalued, culminating in the inevitable downfall. The lesson was duly learned. This is why for many years the shares in the publishing companies of the late Robert Maxwell could be bought for a lower price than might have been presumed from their price/earnings ratio. This discounting of the price was attributed to the 'Maxwell Factor'. The volatility and unpredictability of charismatic individuals creates less confidence than the known solidity of a sound organization. Even admired individual entrepreneurs no longer gain the same confidence that they once did. The charismatic Richard Branson, founder of the Virgin empire, felt the need to buy back shares in his own companies on the grounds that they were undervalued by the market.

Over time there has been a movement in opinion away from backing an heroic leader towards supporting a balanced and effective management team. In effect what has evolved is a newer form of social organization now recognized as offering better long-term survival prospects.

Experimenting with the future

The character of any management system with its soft rather than hard features is difficult to define and more difficult still to communicate to third parties. Yet managers are often quick to recognize the distinctive features of the culture of the company or institution to which they belong, to recognize beneficial advantages of what they see elsewhere and to transfer any lessons they may have learned. Experience counts, yet fashions in management thinking also involve attitudes: they can appeal and vanish as rapidly as a new style in clothing.

The speed at which matters move was brought home to me just after I had finished writing *Team Roles at Work* but before its publication. The last chapter dealt with Organization at a time when I had just begun to formulate my ideas. A model I had postulated was Trapezium Organization. Trapezium in this context represents two-tier Organization, the top tier comprising strategic management and the lower operational management. The trapezium shape resulted from removing a slice at the apex of the triangle to make it flat

Such Organization would be less hierarchical at the top than lower down. I had explained the need for this on the grounds that higher management was often having to deal with highly complex issues. In such situations consultation, along with the pooling and exchange of ideas, tended to pay off well. At the operational level, however, a manager could afford to make more personal decisions, and while teamwork could still be important it was less critical.

I had been invited to give a number of lunchtime talks just before the book appeared and had therefore been in a position to discuss this organizational model. It was a matter of surprise to hear from the third occasion onwards the comment: 'Our company has already introduced Trapezium Organization.' This seemed more than a coincidence, especially as several participants were unsure of the geometric properties of a trapezium!

Due to their abstract and often contentious nature, experiments with Organization are very difficult to get started. But once momentum has been established, ideas spread rapidly. The demand arises because managerial systems, being able to cross technological barriers, enjoy a certain universality in application.

The position is more complicated in the public sector. What constitutes progress is debatable. Objectives are multifaceted. There is no single bottom line. Ideas can seldom be examined in a dispassionate environment, for the issues touch on deeply held sentiments. Any prospect of departure from the familiar is almost certain to encounter opposition. Even so, in the long run the benefits of systems underlining progress made in the private sector eventually transfer to the public sector, as has been shown in recent years in the outsourcing of supply services. Nevertheless the shape of Organization in relation to the functions of the State involves consideration of a number of complex and specific issues. These will be addressed in a later chapter.

I have indicated some of the reasons why small-scale experiments can have far-reaching consequences. The future can now be approached proactively, whereas in the past it was treated passively. But before one can arrive at any conclusions or recommendations, it would be as well to examine where the problems lie.

2

The faltering organization ──────

There was a time when leading corporations in the world received regular accolades from writers and teachers in management for the excellence of their management practices. After all, there was a certain logic in this. If a corporation is successful, it can presumed to be well managed.

Around the time of the second major post-war recession a number of the most famous corporations showed a sudden and remarkable downturn in their fortunes. Then the tone of the comment changed. Some pundits who had been caught out reached for their pens, or word processors, with a view to salvaging their professional reputations through the discovery of hindsights. For other observers of the scene, the episode opened a new debate in the mind which eventually transferred into the agenda of management thinking. Why was the corporation sinking? Could it be that the corporation was comparable with some elegant liner or ocean ferry possessing all the facilities that modernity can offer but nonetheless subject to a serious, and hitherto unnoticed, structural fault?

When a vessel sinks, those in key positions often hasten to disclaim responsibility. But that only increases the mystery. Something evidently is very wrong. But what is it? A lot of people began to wonder.

At a superficial level there is no mystery in the eyes of many members of the public or among those who entertain with comic parody that there is something fundamentally amiss, even though the problem is usually expressed in personal terms. Officials and complacent employees whose actions are governed by the rulebook and who are averse to common sense are regularly lampooned. As a consequence the outsize organization is portrayed as behaving stupidly because it contains stupid people.

When searching for more cogent explanations, opinions become divided. There is one school of thought which attributes lack of responsibility and sensible judgement to the rise of the dependency culture. The growth of an all-pervasive government has removed a clear bottom line in financial accountability while the effects of taxation have reduced personal incentives and the opportunities to create wealth. Another, psychologically based, view explains the shortcomings of organizations on the characteristics of people who seek safe employment. According to this standpoint, the bureaucratic mind is attracted to certain types of job. That is why types of people congregate in particular types of employment. A third interpretation is that behaviour is affected by size of organization, that small is beautiful and that beyond a certain size units fail to function well.

All these contentions have their supporters. But they still leave us with an unanswered question: how is it that people who are individually sensible fail to act sensibly when they get together? If that were properly understood, action could begin to make the world a better place. This is a problem that deserves to be looked at a little more closely.

The idiot organization

One definition of a bureaucrat is that it is a person who inhabits a bureaucracy, where the emphasis is 'to do things right, not to do the right thing'. A bureaucratic mind, on this reckoning, is not in origin a personal trait characterizing an inflexible person but a characteristic of a disciplined employee who takes cognizance of established rules and applies them in the prescribed way. Many officials possess an all-embracing understanding of the rules but are equally adept at knowing how they can legitimately be avoided. Public tax officials commonly come into this category. Eventually their expertise becomes so well developed that they leave the public sector in order to advise private companies.

Bureaucracy is often associated with government. Nevertheless experience suggests that it is not confined to government but is characteristically found in association with organizations operating particular types of rules whether in the public arena or not.

A common phenomenon is the rush to use up a budget before the end of the financial year on the grounds that the budget would be cut next year if the money were not used up. In our own office in Cambridge we never cease to be amazed at the burgeoning of our sales of Interplace, the human resource management system which we despatch to many parts of the world, during the month of March, commonly the last month of the financial year. Video Arts, our partners in the making of industrial films, tell a similar story. There is one month in the year when the bureaucracies of public and private corporations yield a bonanza.

It is understandable that functionaries of a corporation will use up all the money assigned to a particular budget irrespective of need. A reciprocal form of maladaptive behaviour is that executives will defer the purchase of something they need because it has first to go through an elaborate budgeting procedure. In respect to our own office we have noted how a limousine of executives will arrive for a demonstration and display enthusiasm in arriving at a purchasing decision; but nothing will be heard of any order for many months. By contrast, an executive from a small enterprise or a lone consultant will tend to purchase and walk away with a capital item at the first visit, when a favourable view is taken of the item in question. It must be the system that accounts for these two sets of behaviours.

Sometimes the injunction against purchasing a capital item can be conveniently circumvented. For example, one large multinational explained to our office that they were debarred from making a purchase due to a freeze on capital expenditure. However, with a training course due in the near future an inquiry was made into the alternative possibility of buying a set of computer outputs. While that was not part of our regular business, a figure was quoted which the inquirer accepted. The order was thereupon expanded. It emerged that many trainees were passing through a series of training courses. Our office advised that it would be more economic for them to buy the system itself than to pay for a large number of outputs without having anything permanent to show for that expenditure. That advice was set aside. The rules had to be followed and the personal viewpoint of those operating the rules was irrelevant. It was not the individuals who had taken leave of their senses in these cases. Rather it is the rules themselves that are mindless.

These experiences and their counterparts will no doubt be familiar in many businesses. Common sense is not a quality for which provision is made in bureaucracies.

However, the problem can take on even more extreme forms than the cases quoted above. A nonsense can not only be tolerated but may be treated with unwarranted respect. In our office we have had repeated experiences of invoices being paid twice, in effect the converse of the problem of the late payer. A company first declares that accounts will be settled by direct payment into a bank account. While that procedure will be adhered to, a cheque will be sent in response to a demand for an overdue payment so that as a result the bill is paid twice. Such errors or oversights are not in themselves surprising. What is more surprising is the failure of the debtors to acknowledge the error or for them to find a procedure whereby the overpayment can be returned. It was pointed out on one occasion that to accept a return payment a purchase order would need to be raised and it was difficult to find an acceptable procedure for doing this. While bureaucracies have been fashioned with the presumed intention of protecting the interests of the corporation, they often end up acting against their own self-interest because the rules have developed a life of their own.

The reason why sensible people act in a senseless manner must reflect defectiveness in the organization itself. Such defectiveness will be perceived by the outsider. But sometimes it is even more apparent to those on the inside than many people realize.

Insiders have a way of bringing sense back into the system by learning how best to circumvent the rules. It is a consideration that is always worth bearing in mind whenever dealing with officialdom in the British public service. The typical public servant in Britain prides himself or herself on a high standard of personal integrity, respect for the rules and policies devised by the political directorate, and the exercise of intelligence and common sense in their application. If an application is made for a licence, which at first sight is unlikely to be granted, the public servant who is persuaded that the goal would not conflict with the public interest will often advise on how that goal may be achieved. After proper consultation a perfectly acceptable means may be found for meeting the objective in a roundabout way that would never have been evident to the applicant.

In the private sector a readiness to flout the rules without actually infringing them is often handled more directly. Where the sum of money on the face value of a cheque exceeds the amount sanctioned for the immediate removal of a purchased article, the problem is soon solved. Two cheques are presented. That circumvention of the rules has become almost normal procedure. Cheating the system has become good fun. It is not the sort of cheating that commonly appears to create a sense of guilt. The saying that 'it is better to fiddle fools than fight them' applies as much to foolish organizations as to foolish individuals, and perhaps even more.

Erosion of the organization creates a surprise success

For a long time, these observed anomalies were treated as unintended contributors to the fun of living. They were not taken seriously as being any reflection on the health of the corporation as such. Then something happened. An unexpected outcome of the second great recession was the benefit of the almost wanton destruction of organizations that had once acted as models. How many angels can stand on the end of a pin was a metaphysical question that had proved almost as mind-boggling as the issue of how may subordinates should report to a single boss. In Roman times the number was ten, although even the Roman army had difficulty in keeping to the formula. Still the formula was passed on even after the Roman Empire had ceased to exist. By the later stages of the Industrial Revolution the ideal number for industry had moved to, or towards, five on the grounds that subordinates who talk back take up more time. The ideal number was always being debated by the spirited advocates of various schools of management theory. Finally, interest and debate on the ideal number was virtually abandoned as the military model of Organization took a serious knock.

The background to the events that brought this change in climate was the combination of a growing tax imposition on employers, in respect of its employees, and the effect of increased competition, due to the liberalization of international trade, on costs. These two forces generated pressures in the same direction. The urgency to reduce the labour costs of operations became paramount in the deliberations of management, overshadowing all other considerations.

Downsizing now became the order of the day. Downsizing knocked people off the employment roll and at first took the form of random pruning. Voluntary redundancies were invited and this drew volunteers from all departments, generating an imbalance in the shape of the labour force and in the structure of management.

Then a more systematic way of downsizing was introduced: it was known as delayering. Reducing the number of tiers in an organization generated savings in personnel. While that appears to have been the primary reason for engaging in the undertaking, the discovery of the era was that delayered organizations performed better than the organizations that preceded them. The fact that there was now a restriction in the size of the human resources to carry out the functions of supervision and of management proved no disadvantage.

This happy set of benefits – a saving in personnel costs and an improvement in the services rendered to customers and / clients – reopened, in the minds of some, the subject of the ideal shape of an organization. In effect, management theory with its formal models of 'command and control' had now been put in some disarray. This disturbance to long-cherished theories produced a disequilibrium to which some solution had to be found.

One solution was to abandon command and to rely on control. While some corporations on a downwards slide tried varied means of improving their management grip, certain other corporations were moving ahead in their field. These were the companies whose strategies were based on financial control with no pretence to 'managing' the companies they owned.

Their basic strategies were simple. Buy a financially stagnant company but one with good assets or with a well established demand for their products. Remove the top management apart from one or two with special flair or skills. Sell off assets surplus to the core business. Give middle management the opportunity to manage. Provide them with the tools for the job. Make the management responsible for generating a reasonable return on assets and give them a personal incentive. Then leave them to it. If they failed, others could be found to take their place.

These apostles of financial management, dubbed by some of their critics as asset strippers, made no pretence about developing new forms of management organization. They did not figure on the management lecturing circuit, nor did they profess any interest in management theory, nor did they talk about such metaphysical subjects as human motivation. Yet in practice they found themselves taking over companies that housed admired centres of management teaching, often in hostile bids. The progress of these financial strategists could hardly have been more eloquent testimony to the fact that commonly accepted notions of organizational effectiveness were in decline, for in practice those who held them were unable to hold their own in the assaults on their strongholds.

A phoenix from the ashes

The thinkers in management may have had a setback. Yet it was not long before they began to show signs of recovery. They realized that a change in the recommended span of control would have a funda-mental effect on the processes of management. Some traditional practices were bound to become obsolete. Attitudes had to change. Flatter organizations meant that fewer would be engaged in the business of 'commanding and controlling'. The emphasis therefore switched to better self regulation by peers which could only be accomplished by improved teamwork.

For a time teamwork became the order of the day. But it did not prove a panacea. After a while it became apparent that some teams were inward-looking and prone to complacency. They were happy but ineffective. Now a new organizational strategy began to emerge. Instead of having a given number of individuals reporting to a boss, teams could be substituted for individuals. In that way a small number of senior people could be offered a wide span of responsibility in a generally flatter organization. All that was needed was to find managers of sufficient calibre with a capacity for a broad overview.

So, as middle managers were ousted from their jobs, a scramble began to find top managers who could run slimmed down organiza-tions and make the key decisions. The work of 'head hunters' (also known by their more discreet title as those engaged in Executive Search) grew in importance. With the right person in supreme command, a leaner organization and fewer middle managers, the theory was that the corporation would outperform competitors.

So the hunt began for individuals of 'sufficient size' who could match the challenge of the new scenario. A new era of management learning was set in motion. But some of this learning was eventually to involve a good deal of agony.

3

The problem with Mr Big ─────

People are very ready to press the case for good leadership, a matter that leads on to the form that leadership should take and the personal qualities that should be embodied in a good leader. Sight is soon lost of the fact that the notion of a leader draws in its wake the need for followers.

The concept of leadership soon becomes associated with a Mr Big. Only occasionally is there a Mrs Big, and, more rarely still, a Miss Big. The idealized Mr Big has the qualities of the heroic leader: whether those qualities exist or not is another matter.

The acceptance of 'bigness' would seem to derive from a fundamental human tendency to look for and revere someone of supreme importance whether at the religious, political or business levels.

The Incas of South America, the Pharaohs of Egypt, the Popes of Rome, the Dalai Lamas of Tibet and the Emperors of Japan offer examples of figures who were not only powerful but whose sanctity gave them immunity against rational challenge and argument. Institutions consolidate the position of religious leaders, for it is the office of the leader, no less than the person, that commands reverence. Appointment at the summit is for life. Personal ability, or the lack of it, has no bearing on fitness to continue in office. Religious leaders who lack the backing of long-established institutions, and belong in the power sense to a second league, need to display more proactive qualities. This would seem to demand personal charisma and the creation of a mystique; but the effect can be mesmeric. Some fringe cults have produced leaders remarkably effective in bringing about compliance: their followers have even engaged in mass suicides at their leader's bidding.

Political leaders also need a mechanism for bringing about followership. Those who have seized power and lack a democratic mandate have a propensity for conferring high-sounding titles on themselves. By this and other means they cultivate the awe more often associated with religious leaders. The measure of their success in so doing is their capacity for retaining the devotion of huge numbers of followers even when they have led their countries to semi-ruin. Clearly their rise, along with the maintenance of their position, is attributable to certain psychogenic forces that they can manipulate in their favour rather than to a high level of general personal ability.

For political leaders who operate in a democratic system, a different situation prevails, for the pressures are greater and are multifaceted. Admirers are balanced by ever-present detractors. Continuation in office requires a large measure of political and all-round skills.

The ingrained tendency for people to look for and to follow a leader can be observed in many spheres of life and prompts two related questions: how far can this tendency, if properly harnessed, be treated as an asset for the running of a business? Conversely, are the consequences of the Big Leader and mass follower syndrome likely to prove damaging to the long-term interests of the corporation?

The rise and rise of the Big Leader

In business and industry the possession of a high level of ability is indispensable in the leadership function. There is a consensus that outstanding mental ability (covering intellect, imagination and vision), a relentless drive and a capacity for self-projection are valued qualities. Potential leaders also need to prove themselves on the way up. In a society where performance counts, and where it can be assessed on some acknowledged basis of accomplishment, and where there are many contenders for the top job, the Big Leader is bound to have some justifiable claim to bigness.

An ingrained tendency to follow a powerful leader with charisma rather than broadly based talents may have many disastrous consequences in certain fields of human affairs. But in the world of business and industry, real merit counts. A person in a key position who fails to live up to expectations becomes very vulnerable and is apt to be summarily dismissed.

The value attached to the appointment of the Big Leader in business and industry can be gauged by the level of salaries paid at the highest level. Booms and recessions have scarcely changed the position. There used to be an argument in times of greater industrial stability that high salaries at the top were justified on the grounds of creating 'headroom'. This meant that an appropriate set of incentives for career development could be created at every level. In a multi-tiered organization it followed that at the summit the top salary had to be fully commensurate with the position.

Now that organizations have been delayered, often for economic reasons, that argument has collapsed. So one might have expected that top salaries would fall; or rather that the rate of increase would decline. Yet examination of trends suggests the reverse has been happening. Pay differentials for positions at the summit, in so far as they have moved at all, have been increasing. So what is the explanation?

A flaw in cultural congruence

This question had puzzled me for some time. Flatter organizations suggest flatter salaries. But perhaps the issue can be looked at from another angle.

I stumbled upon a possible answer as a result of a questionnaire devised for some seminars I was running and of the responses they generated. My belief had been that a teamworking culture and hierarchical decision-making were likely to be inversely related. Put another way, teams imply the sharing of power and the reduction of autocracy. But the point needed to be checked. I had asked the participants at the seminars to use ratings on a scale of 1–9 on two issues. One related to the extent to which they engaged in unstructured work, where work boundaries and responsibilities were negotiated between associates; in other words this scale provided an index of a teamworking culture. The other dimension related to the extent to which groups were empowered to make decisions on the issues that fell within their orbit. The exercise was one way of steering discussion into organizational forms.

What emerged was that the ratings on the two scales formed no particular pattern. That was not what I had expected. Further questioning brought home the point that some firms priding them- selves on their teamwork and employee participation possessed very hierarchical decision-making processes. In contrast, there were firms in which employees were slotted into highly structured jobs but where management made decisions by consensus and consultation.

There is always the problem that if two distinct cultures become mixed, the result produces the worst features of both worlds. Teamwork, or rather lip service to teamwork, had become very fashionable and a number of corporations had adopted this approach at the behest of their training departments, while at the same time their management structures retained their typically authoritarian character. This hybrid can bring about a great deal of wasted effort.

The nature of the problem was brought home to me in connection with a company engaged in new product development with which I had a close association. A large conglomerate operating in the defence field was seeking diversification following a downturn in its core business with the ending of the Cold War. The new product development company had gained the attention of one part of the conglomerate. Several meetings were held between the two parties, a proposal was approved, market research generated encouragement for the pursuit of a new product and a prototype was finally developed. A plan for funding the next stage now had to be submitted to the headquarters of the conglomerate. The response came back rapidly: launch of the new product would not go ahead and the plan was dropped. The supply company was frustrated by the final decision of a Group Finance Director, who had never attended earlier discussions and whose crucial position had never been mentioned.

Teams that are not empowered to act on their decisions are frequently overruled by a (sometimes unseen) member of the hierarchy. The deployment of a powerful individual in this way can scarcely constitute efficiency. The question must therefore be asked: how it is that such a mixed culture, lacking the strengths of its progenitors, can arise in a corporation?

The origin of the apparent anomaly of a cultural mix between a team culture and a hierarchy dominated by a solo leader can be explained easily enough. One of the merits of the old multi-tiered organization was that every decision-making executive had a manageable span of responsibility. Even if an overview might be lacking and decisions were fragmented, decisions were at least spread between managers who had enough time to handle them. In effect, managers often ran their own fiefdoms. But a consequence of the removal of tiers in the hierarchy and of the downgrading of the fiefdoms has been a rejigging in the balance of power and decision-making. The growing flatness in organizational shape has given rise to what at first sight may seem contradictory effects. Interest in teamwork has often gone hand in hand with a renewed emphasis on what is termed leadership. The implication here is the added importance of finding a person with the requisite size and breadth to take on an extended span of responsibility.

The assets and liabilities of bigness

The growth of cultural teamwork in a flatter corporation, if unaccompanied by organizational reform, is likely to increase the separation between those engaged in the everyday work of the corporation and those who wield the levers of power. A slim top management is currently in favour. Companies often take a pride in having a small head office with low attendant costs. The price that has to be paid for this economy is the rise of an oligarchy. Bigger decisions are made by a smaller number of people – sometimes by a single person.

Talent is always welcome and the bigger the level of responsibility the more welcome it becomes. The fact that some tycoons possess outstanding talent cannot be doubted. However, top leaders in business and industry, unlike those in religion and politics, cannot count on faith or coercion to act on their behalf; they have usually had to struggle for their positions on the basis of skills that are shown to surpass those of their competitors. If a corporation is to succeed, there is therefore an understandable argument in favour of appointing an outstanding person with a proven record to run it and giving that person the necessary power and the scope, along with responsibility for the outcome. A belief in that approach has its political counterparts. Critics of democracy often declare that a society is best run by a benevolent despot.

There are a few examples of Solo Leaders who have lived up to expectations of this kind. Yet many Solo Leaders with illustrious beginnings finish badly and sadly, for they have an especially poor record in handling their exit from the throne. Management succession raises issues that they often refuse to face. The result is that the work of the former leader may be overturned completely by the next incumbent. Whatever the level of temporary success, the opportunities that are seized when a talented Solo Leader takes charge have to be balanced against the subsequent damage. The effectiveness of the organization as a whole is often reduced, together with the capacity for charting a way forward into the future.

I have had a number of opportunities of studying the behaviour of Big Leaders in business at first hand. Nearly all of them possess immense talents. But the troubles that beset them in one way or another are no less conspicuous.

Mr Big never feels comfortable unless in total control. Mr Big likes to know everything that is going on, while, by contrast, others around Mr Big are left in the dark and spend part of their time guessing. Mr Big shows equal interest in the strategic side of the business and the operational side. Nothing is allowed to escape his gaze. As a result Mr Big is overworked. The fact that Mr Big is a workaholic and often arrives at the office before anyone else would appear to be an adaptation to the intensities of the work load. But the harder Mr Big works, the greater the work load becomes. That is because Mr Big generates much work for his staff. The outcomes of his briefings and instructions then need to be supervised, for Mr Big refuses to believe that others can be left on their own and are bright enough to make the right decisions. The in-tray is always full. A comment about one Chief Executive of a large corporation from a close associate that the organization 'has been designed to meet his personal emotional needs' becomes understandable. Mr Big, being overworked, is always under strain.

The consequence of this style of working is that Mr Big inevitably makes blunders, sometimes blunders of commission but more often of omission. That is not because of any lack of cerebral capacity or temperamental instability, although these can, where they occur, introduce their own specific set of difficulties. The problem is more basic than that since it is prone to affect even the most talented Chief Executive. It arises from what is known as the psycho-physiological bottleneck.

The limits of attention

Psycho-physiology covers attention-span, reaction-times and single channel capacity. A great deal is known about these fields through the work of the experimental psychologists. Put simply, the importance of this subject area means that only one thing can be attended to at a time; the bigger the range of choices, the longer decision-making takes. Some activities can be automated in such a way that they create no conflict on attention. Talking and knitting can be carried on simultaneously. But if a stitch is dropped, conversation is interrupted.

The time taken to respond to items that necessitate separate discrimination increases exponentially in reaction-time experiments. The formula for that increase can be expressed mathematically. It is unrelated to intelligence. Quite apart from speed of reaction, that is of thinking, attention cannot be paid to two separate matters simultaneously. Again, this is not a matter of intelligence. It is a limitation imposed by the physiological design of the human nervous system.

The central nervous system has an integrated system of command and control not unlike the workings of the organization chart associated with formal hierarchies. The two systems have an affinity that seems more than a coincidence. And one suspects a common origin. The chart that depicts individual decision-making almost serves to represent the decision-making processes of the organization. The same bottleneck arises at the summit. In the case of the individual, it is the queue for attention by the cerebral cortex: in the case of the organization, it is the size of the pile on the in-tray of the Chief Executive's desk.

The closeness of the two systems in terms of how they operate can be illustrated by taking a practical example of the handling of events leading up to the Falklands War. The British Navy had withdrawn a naval vessel which protected the islands. That action, it seems, was interpreted by the authorities in Buenos Aires as acquiescence by the British Government to the claim of the Argentinians to the islands and a green light for them to go ahead. That improbable interpretation did not occur to the British Government which at the time was preoccupied with a Middle East crisis. Intelligence reports indicated that the Argentinians were preparing an invasion. That information was patent enough for it to be reported in some sections of the British press and must also certainly have been picked up by the Intelligence officials of Ministries. However, the message had to get through the barrier of lesser officials and it seems was eventually relegated to a low position on the agenda of the Cabinet. Allegedly the matter did not

What is the common bottleneck?

Answer: The brain lies at the top of the central nervous system and the 'brain' that makes all the important decisions at the top of the large organizations are subject to the same limitations. Restriction in attention span and the time available to process inputs become the inevitable consequences of 'single-channel capacity'.

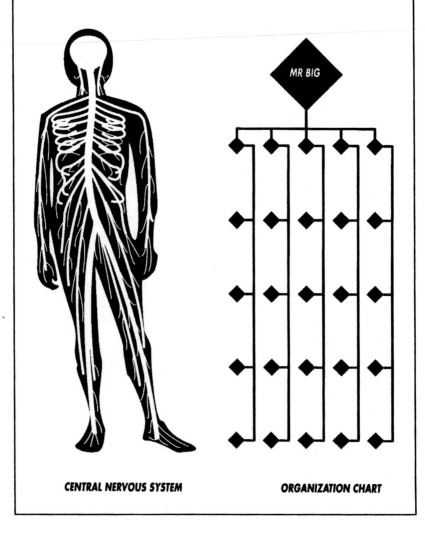

CENTRAL NERVOUS SYSTEM   **ORGANIZATION CHART**

reach the conscious attention of Margaret Thatcher until the invasion had started. The war therefore was triggered off in the first place by incompetence, that is by the inability of the system to cope with the Big Leader's in-tray. In the event, that failure rebounded into an electoral success for Margaret Thatcher who became the heroine of the crisis as soon as the invasion was defeated. The incompetence of the Argentinian generals, along with a failure in the trigger mechanism of the bombs that fell on British naval vessels, outstripped the incompetence of the style of leadership which Thatcher provided. When one incompetence outweighs another the result can be positive.

The Second World War offers an even more startling example of the failure of the Big Leader to cope with the in-tray. The most brilliant spy of the war was Sorge, a former German Communist, who had managed to get into a senior position in the German Embassy in Tokyo. Sorge provided the Kremlin with precise details of the forthcoming German invasion of Russia. The message was in the system but the Big Leader never acted on it.

The theory of the single-channel capacity makes it plain why this will always happen when organizations, like human beings, are subject to information overload at the system's summit. However, inadequate capacity is not the only reason for the breakdown of hierarchical systems at or around the summit. It is not just a question of attention capacity but of attention direction.

The Big Leader is in the position of choosing to attend to parts of the information field that appeal and to ignore other parts that are less attractive. The greater the tendency for a venture to become the personal toy of the Big Leader or to be bound up with the Big Leader's personal reputation, the more selective becomes the nature of the attention. Negative information deriving from early financial returns or from market research will tend to be ignored. The bottleneck then becomes not information overload, but a refusal to face the facts or to form the inevitable conclusion that the facts suggest. It is perhaps for this reason that the biggest disasters I have encountered in corporations have been associated with the presence of the Big Leader who in earlier stages of his career had enjoyed a tremendous run of success.

Finally there is a third category of attention-related problems attaching to the Big Leader who has a hand in all that is going on, who assigns work but not responsibility and is liable to overrule anyone. The problem is that of tempo. Individuals have their own characteristic tempo of working. That becomes a problem only when attention needs to be given to matters that are better handled at two distinct levels of tempo. Operational issues usually call for quick-wittedness and decisive action, while strategic issues demand patient investigation and depth of thought. The Big Leader who scores on the first area is inclined to fall short in attention-supply when the second area comes into focus. High mental ability provides some measure of compensation but response to what this field demands is still likely to be sub-optimal. The Big Leader is short of time. And it shows.

The leader or the organization: which comes first?

When power is more broadly spread at the top, mistakes are easier to rectify. This is because ownership of ventures is less personalized. One person in a team may back a particular venture but when it fails to fulfil expectations there will be another to propose that it is shut down. Since the outside world will not associate the venture with a particular person, no-one in the team is made to feel especially vulnerable or blameworthy.

The Big Leader on the other hand builds up such a personal reputation that no single reverse can be endured. The way in which the Big Leader operates and the way in which the organization functions cannot therefore be separated. The organization has to function in the Big Leader's image.

The concept of the Big Leader, as it has been treated in this chapter, will no doubt differ from the sort of real leadership that has been written about or advocated in management schools. The reason for writing as I have is that I have drawn a picture of leaders of corporations as I have observed them. I have resisted seduction into writing about ideal leaders who exist in the abstract but are rarely seen. Yet I must confess that there are one or two leaders I have encountered who correspond to the ideal pattern and who have enjoyed uninterrupted success. Their names however are largely unknown to the general public, or, even where they are known, these leaders are inclined to make themselves inconspicuous. This reluctance springs primarily from a focus on the team itself and on teamwork. Instead of assuming personal credit for what is achieved, the credit is spread to colleagues and contributors. The true Big Leader does not claim to be big or to appear so. It is size of another kind: it has to do with personal maturity.

When a corporation looks to the future and to the challenges that lie ahead, the first thought is usually to declare: how shall we be led? Who possesses a talent commensurate with the size of the task? Perhaps an alternative set of questions is better raised: what sort of organization do we need? Which people are better fitted to contribute to its various but interacting parts? And can that leadership function, which is expected by the many, be spread without being in any way weakened?

4

Lessons from a diminutive masterclass ———————

Most large-scale human organizations spawn either bureaucracy and inertia or, at the political level, intolerance and aggression towards dissidents or outsiders. Very often some combination of both can be detected. Organizations which prove the exceptions are usually more amorphous in form; and hence their weaknesses are of a different character, for they tend to be innocuous and effete, especially where their functions and ambitions are limited.

These generalizations about the shortcomings of human organizations are not absolute but are relative to size. Very large organizations do not behave in the same way as the fairly large. Medium-sized organizations show their inadequacies to a much lesser degree. And as one proceeds down the size scale the situation changes in a favourable direction. Numerous small human groups have proved wonderfully creative, dynamic and cohesive in many fields of endeavour and this no doubt accounts for the widely held belief that 'small is beautiful'.

If one turns that aphorism on its head to give us 'big is ugly', some demanding questions then arise. Why should that be? Are big organizations always ugly? Or is it only big human organizations that show their ugliness? To answer those questions we need to look at ourselves as if from the outside.

One way in which humans have always endeavoured to learn, when confronted by barriers to progress, is to see what nature can tell us. In the field of medicines pioneers have searched through the rich diversity of plants in jungles to discover those with special properties that, once discovered, can be synthesized. The pioneers of aviation, too, were inspired by the realization that other creatures discovered flight before humans. The shape of wings in providing lift for birds was found to apply to wings (the very same name) of planes, demonstrating again that other creatures arrived there first.

When it comes to social organization and behaviour appropriate to domestic living, humans have always taught or, more exactly, trained animals. The teaching has never been the other way round. It is almost inconceivable that the more intelligent should be taught by the less intelligent. Or could it be that there is a myth here founded on a conceit? Is it possible that other creatures have first discovered the secret of how to run large organizations?

A buzzing organization with something to teach

Civilization is a very recent phenomenon relative to the protracted social development and evolution of *Homo sapiens*. The very word civilization derives from the culture produced by citizens of the city. Towns and cities call for sophisticated social behaviour. While human towns and cities have been in existence for only a few thousand years, other creatures got there before us. The true pioneers of towns and cities go back several million years.

The first master-builders of civilization were bees and termites. The former have established the skills for constructing towns comprising several thousand inhabitants; while the latter have built cities of sophisticated design, with tower blocks and subterranean chambers, animal ranching for the supply of fresh food and a wide range of luxuries including, amid the harshness of the Australian climate, air conditioning. All these impressive accomplishments demand and depend on a highly sophisticated system of work organization.

The secrets of the underlying design of these civilizations have only come to light in recent years and even now are not as fully understood as one might wish. The first of these civilizations to engage detailed attention was that of the honey bee. The reason, no doubt, is that the production of honey plus the role of the bee in pollinating flowers in orchards were matters of economic importance.

So how do bees organize themselves? Certainly the reality is different from some popular conceptions. The world of bees and ants has often conjured up a picture full of anthropomorphic overtones. The centre of the bee world, just like the ant world, is the queen, a word implying an imperious figure surrounded by obedient servants. The Red Queen in *Alice Through the Looking Glass* spent much of her time exclaiming: 'Off with their heads.'

The real bee queen is, by contrast, no ruler but a mainly passive creature with a limited behavioural repertoire and a smaller brain than worker bees. Her bellicosity is reserved solely for other potential queen bees. Otherwise her role is that of a specialized breeding machine. The worker bees that surround the queen are not fawning courtiers but bees engaged in a necessary two-way exchange that operates in the interests of the hive as a whole: the queen receives food and the (female) workers receive pheromones (chemical agents affecting behaviour) which contribute to the inhibition of worker ovary development. In that way the population is stabilized and conflict between queens is avoided. Should the queen die and so lose her inhibitory influence, a mechanism is in place which will lead to the emergence of new queens.

The organization of bee 'towns' does not depend on hierarchy: the queen is not a ruler and there are no foremen to organize the worker bees. Another misconception is that, in the absence of intelligence, bees act from blind instinct in the performance of the complex tasks required in the construction, maintenance and provision of services to a town. Simple and undirected reflexes cannot manage complexity or account for the highly adaptive social response of bees to the wide variety of hazards that can threaten their colony.

So how do bees do it? They appear to have developed a finely tuned system of communication based on a distinctive set of organizational principles. Like humans, bees are programmed to engage in different sorts of activity that peak at different ages in the life-span. Here there are both similarities and differences. Infant humans engage in imitative behaviour. As children, they love to memorize and are fond of nursery rhymes; as adolescents, they focus on vigorous physical activities; they move on to an interest in decision-making and problem-solving and in later years, typically, to the cultivation of gardens. During the earliest days of life bees are most likely to be engaged in cleaning cells and in the last days of working life in foraging. One study identifies fourteen different tasks in which worker bees engage. Yet while each task is most likely to be performed within a particular age span, the range of ages at which bees are known to perform particular work can be wide. This is worth thinking about in the context of the general capacity for organization.

It appears that while the choice of tasks on which to engage depends on individual bee maturation and on the development of a bee's glands, it is not the only factor influencing the choice of bee occupation. Research has established that the tasks that need doing can determine the condition of a bee's glands. For example, disturbance to the nest or moving the queen will activate a new set of activities and bring about changes in the physical condition of the bees. Individual bee 'decisions' can introduce another set of factors that impinge on the community. Bee behaviour is influenced by temperature and light. Bees that 'decide' to station themselves at the periphery of the nest are more likely to engage in tasks atypical for the age of those particular bees and that may partly account for the wide diversity of tasks undertaken by bees of any particular age. Finally account needs to be taken of the highly social nature of bees, for they are attracted to each other by sight, vibration, heat and odour. They communicate with each other by gesture and dance. A bee that begs will demand and receive food from another bee. In what appears an altruistic and community-based service bees that find a source of food will return to the nest to recruit other bees in order to join in the foraging. The location of the food is spelt out with some precision by a dance.

Besides the queen bee, the sterile worker bees and the larvae, the nest contains a smaller number of male bees termed drones which spend the greater part of their life in idleness. But research shows that if the nest comes under stress, so that there is a shortage of labour, the drones start taking over some of the tasks normally undertaken by the worker bees. The drones are similar, in an economic sense, to the unemployed in human society: given the appropriate conditions, they act as a reserve labour force.

Altogether, bees have a set of interlocking systems that act together to produce stability. The core of that stability depends not on reflex activities to given stimuli but on an intricate system of social communication that is part gestural and part chemical in nature.

The organizing genius of ants and termites

The phrase 'as busy as a bee' would seem a little overstated if account is taken of the idleness of the drones, together with other periods when bees are observed to be resting in the nest. If bees are busy, then busier still is the ant. Whereas the nests of bees contain a lot of standard housing, ants construct elaborate towns, containing tunnels, galleries and chambers, built from materials that vary with the situation and with designs that are well adapted to the location. Further, ants are the world's pioneers when it comes to 'dairy farming', 'cattle raising' and 'agriculture'. More than three thousand species of insects have been recorded as being harboured in ant colonies for one reason or another. Aphids, leaf-hoppers and larvae of small butterflies are kept for the sweet secretions they produce and are 'milked' like cows. Conspicuous on the agricultural front are the fungus-growers. While some ants cultivate the fungus garden, other ants go forth to cut fresh leaves and so provide the cellulose needed to meet the metabolic needs of the growing crop. The fungus itself enriches the diet of the ant community by compensating for dietary deficiencies to which the ant community is subject. Otherwise foraging acts as the main source of food supply but even here some division of labour assists the efficiency of the process. Some ants forage outside for seeds which are then brought in and passed on to other ants whose job is to crush them. The distribution of food is then assisted by one simple means in that an ant adopting a begging posture will be duly rewarded by a provider ant.

The intricate nature of ant society can be surpassed in the world of nature only, perhaps, by their fellow countrymen in the tropics – the termites. Their high-rise cities, comparable in size of population to those of humans, are built by an array of professional specialists, pillar constructors, horizontal floor builders and other 'tradespeople' whose personal behaviours have yet to be fully studied. There are chimneys for air movements; there are deep wells that reach down to the water table from which termites transport water in their gut so as to moisten the nest; and there are subterranean traps for storing water during the rains. The overall effect of these combined constructions is to provide an assured system of air conditioning in a climate marked by long periods of arid heat. The compass termites of Western Australia have been found to maintain the temperature inside their nest to within one degree around 31 degrees Celsius, day and night, summer and winter – while the external temperature varies between 3 and 42 degrees Celsius. As the towers heat up, the air inside them rises, drawing fresh currents through the termites' living quarters. Additional precision control is made possible by worker termites that regulate the air flow by blocking and unblocking the numerous channels.

The range of 'castes' on which termite society is built extends from the caring to the fearsome. Nurse termites feed the larvae, attend them solicitously, shift their position from hour to hour, help them build their own cocoons when the proper time arrives, and assist in the delicate operation of bringing forth the young perfect insect. Here there is some payment for the nurse's work, for the larvae exude an attractive substance which the nurses lick. At the other end of the scale are very large soldier termites with mandibles so powerful that they have been found to bore into billiard balls. Their role is to protect the small forager termites, which are very vulnerable to predators, as well as to protect the nest.

Perhaps the most spectacular of the soldier castes are the guards that live in cylindrical tunnels which are prone to invasion by raider ants. These guards are known as 'walking bombs', for they have developed a tunnel-blocking form of defence and are capable of bursting their bodies in ejecting the contents of their salivary gland reservoirs in a remarkable act of altruistic suicide.

Another defence requirement is the escape route, and here the importance of saving the queen has given rise to a remarkable example of contingency planning. A tunnel is constructed which leads to a launching pad. If the last defences fail, the queen can be evacuated and a new colony can be started in a safer location.

Ants and termites, like humans, are prone to engage in wars on one another, although at most other times they will treat strangers with cautious respect. Within their own communities cooperation reigns, for they are members of a complete superorganism, expertly fashioned to meet mutual needs. Cooperation is achieved without coercion. Any 'antisocial' individual is free to wander away from the colony and never to return. But under stable conditions behaviour contrary to the social interest is almost unknown, for both the freedom and the security of ants and termites is combined by belonging to a well-balanced community.

Pioneering principles of the superorganism

So how have bees, ants and termites built up their civilization? How is it that they have mastered the principles of large-scale organization before humans, with their supposedly super intelligences, have discovered them?

In order to establish an overview in attempting to answer these questions, it is as well to put aside the boundaries between these diminutive creatures which have made their own forms of adaptation to the pressures upon them; for the reason in writing as I have is not to expound some entomological treatise but merely to extract those principles that account for the remarkable success. Colonial bees, nest-making ants and termites comprise what are now termed the eusocial insects. These can be considered together since evolution has conferred on them the same basic model of organization. If one model is considered rather more than another, it is merely that it has become more sophisticated in its progress down a given evolutionary track.

The first observation about the strength of these advanced communities is that of the division of labour between the castes. A caste is a technical term used by zoologists to differentiate the physical and behavioural differences of individuals within a species. The point is that the relationship is one of interdependence. Each caste fulfils a needed role within the community and there is no caste or class conflict. It is the balance between these castes at any one time, even under widely varying environmental conditions, that gives the community its stability.

The second observation relates to their superior use of intelligence. It is a common attitude to find the intelligence of bees and ants dismissed on the grounds that their behaviour is based solely on blind instinct. That criticism cannot be upheld in relation to their finely attuned responses to the very specific crises that threaten the community from time to time. Nor is lack of intelligence consistent with the well developed brains of ants. Some of their castes have brains that occupy an especially high percentage of their overall body-weight, even to the point of implying the possession of the most advanced intellect of all living species. If we have difficulty in recognizing their intelligence, it is because it operates in a different way from our own. For one thing, the context is different. Humans have a long life. Infants start by knowing nothing and begin their explorations of the world with the sort of blind instincts that humans are prone to give as explanations of the behaviour of bees and ants. Much of the effective intelligence of the maturing human is acquired through cultural transmission over a long period. Some of this transmission actually restricts the range of behaviours and adaptations available as so often occurs in societies built up on some form of religious or political fundamentalism.

The eusocial insects, by contrast, have a shorter life and their intelligence needs to come into play very rapidly. Their brains are fashioned as integrators of information coming from a wider range of senses than humans could possibly handle all at the same time. The perception of odour and taste (senses that humans have difficulty in distinguishing between), touch, sight, the sensing of temperature differences and above all response to the range of pheromones (the chemical agents affecting behaviour) emitted by other castes can all be processed at the same time to result in a form of finely attuned pattern of action. These brains with their rapid integrating functions can be likened more to computers than the brains of humans. The latter are better adapted to single-channel processing, allowing attention to be given to information in only one modality at a time.

A further difference in intelligence relates to its social character among these advanced insects. In the event of a crisis, information in all the modalities is exchanged by a number of individuals, of the right

Table 4.1 A comparison in features of organization between humans and the higher insects

	Humans	Higher insects
Nature of hierarchy	Centralization Individuals oversee and overrule	Devolved nature of operations Some individuals hold more vital jobs than others
Social behaviour	Emphasis on individual gain	Focus on needs of community or colony
Communication	Top down Junk material at other levels	Lateral, elaborate and multi-modal
Speed of response	Delays due to single channel upward referral and to intricate appeal systems in public sector	Rapid reaction force operating locally and containing the necessary specialisms
Source of specialist services	Extended education and training Aptitude obscured by formal qualifications	Castes with genetically appropriate behaviour Conversion of castes to meet perceived needs of situation

Unrelated insects have found similar solutions to similar problems caste, acting in concert so that the information basis for eventual action is cross-linked and very well grounded. With humans, the hierarchical nature of large organizations means that a limited set of information is fed upwards and away from the practitioners; a decision is then eventually made, often by a single person, which is then binding on everyone else. Here the room for error is very large.

A third observation relates to caste which, unlike its meaning in Indian society, is not a totally exclusive category, to which there is no other entry except at birth. The perception of changing need results in some variation in the management of pheromones in the nursing of the larvae. This allows the numbers of certain castes to increase and the numbers of other castes to decline. In other words, those responsible for the upbringing of the young can influence career development in a way that reflects the interests of the community as a whole. In this respect these diminutive tutors are more advanced than teachers in human society. The latter, even in conditions of a rapidly changing labour market, are unaccustomed to varying their teaching material. Hence, their students are taught things for which they will have no ultimate need in the society they ultimately join. In the case of ants and bees, the duality of approach, whereby larvae are born into one caste but may be drafted into another, gives the community great flexibility in adjusting its population to differing external pressures.

The fourth observation relates to the benefits of devolved power whereby ants and bees can engage speedily in intricate reconstruction work in emergencies without resort to the protracted planning and referral procedures that tie up so much human endeavour. The basis of their superior organization lies, first, in the availability of on-the-spot specialists who work together to formulate the shape and nature of group effort in their respective spheres, and, secondly, the existence of a system geared for concurrent activities. There is no chain of command to impede things. For humans, life is far more complicated; they have to take one step at a time. In the case of bees and ants, it can all happen together.

The fifth observation is that the strength and stability of the overall organization lies in the way in which its various sub-systems interlock. There is no single controlling mechanism that can go wrong.

Of ants and men

There is a limit on the extent to which human society can borrow the procedures and systems that go into the building of, for example, an ant hill. The morphologies of ants and men, their rate of growth from infancy and their total life-spans, together with the biologically rooted ways in which the two groups communicate with members of their own kind, all differ too much to enable them to form much of a link with one another. Ants and humans have built their civilizations on a different genetic base.

The behaviour of the eusocial insects generally has been furnished with the same explanation as that applied to the behaviour of mammals by postulating a 'selfish gene'. That does not imply that such a gene has been actually located. It is better understood as a shorthand for saying that the whole genetic complex of an individual animal creates a body and drives its behaviour with the ultimate purpose of protecting and propagating its own genetic complex. Putting it another way, the theory holds that the life of an individual animal is devoted to the perpetuation of his/her genes if necessary at the expense of his/her life. The fact that the vast majority of eusocial insects will forgo reproduction can make evolutionary sense. They are closely related to one another. They are all siblings. Because the queen's genes are their genes, there is no significant loss of genetic material.

However, given the social behaviour of the eusocial insects the essential exclusivity of the term 'selfish gene' does not seem especially apt. One school of socio-biologists has postulated instead another gene, conferring 'social donorism'. Self-destructive behaviour, if of benefit to the colony itself, will have evolved through the natural selection of those colonies best fitted to survive. Evolution is operating more on colonies than on individuals. A gene for 'social donorism' should again be interpreted as referring to actions of the genetic complex itself rather than to one single element of it. On this model there is a case for reconsidering the nature of our society as being made up of eusocial humans rather than individuals.

Human altruistic behaviour, or a capacity for self-sacrifice, is usually attributed to the possession of certain values and beliefs. The willingness of so many people to sacrifice their personal leisure time for flag days in the interest of good causes and for men to rush in as volunteers to lay down their lives 'for their country' suggests that 'social donorism' is a behavioural propensity with genetic foundations that is more widespread than may have been imagined. It may have developed in our own species too, even if it is less developed than in insects.

Whatever the degree of similarity or dissimilarity between species with such different anatomies, the organizational principles that have evolved to give bees, ants and termites a certain superiority in their organizational behaviour can be extracted and adapted for human society; and it is not too much to expect that they could be put into use by the arrival and early beginnings of the twenty-first century. These principles need to be basic, for exactly how they should be put into operation remains another question.

There are two general guidelines that are basic enough to seem worth transferring immediately to human affairs.

The first is that there are better ways of managing a complex organization than by making it the responsibility of a single boss. If a major decision-making function is needed, it should be based on the concept of a cooperating 'caste'. Members of that 'caste' should be selected and trained for the position in the same way as larvae are nurtured by a nurse. Expressed in other words and in human terms, the emerging adult contributor needs to be prepared for the position by a personal development coach. However, the lesson from our diminutive tutors is that to rely on that sole approach would restrict biological adaptability. Others need to be recruited to the 'caste' in accordance with the perception of immediate needs and observed pressures. In effect, the 'caste' should have two sources of entry, one trained from the outset and the other recruited at shorter notice.

The second guideline derives from the observation that a large mass of individual 'castes' function efficiently when their separate but complementary work activities operate simultaneously, in unison and free from the delays associated with relationships of rank. Hence a principle can be deduced that the larger the body corporate, the more important becomes the need for an organization to be built around concurrent systems, differentiated in terms of function and scope, but interlinked rather than separated.

In the chapters that follow I will endeavour to find ways of putting these principles into a practical form and in a way that takes account of the current state of society. I will argue that parallel evolution will almost inevitably take us in the direction of species that have arrived at superior forms of organization before us. But before attention is given to this subject, it is as well to look more closely at where the problems lie in human Organization.

5
Concurrent versus sequential decision-making ———————

When business corporations, or Nation States, have been headed by a Mr Big until disaster has set in, and Mr Big has been recognized as a liability and duly dispatched, what follows next becomes the crucial issue. The problem extends beyond finding a replacement. All Mr Bigs make their personal mark on the organizations they head. The bigger the Mr Big, the closer the personal allegiances that will have been formed and the tighter, and usually the more inflexible too, will be the infrastructure at the base of the organization.

Those who cope with succession planning must decide whether or not to start looking for a more acceptable version of the departed. That conservative way of treating the resulting situation does have certain advantages. Much of what is already intact can be revived and perhaps revitalized. The usual reaction, however, is to turn the ship's tiller in the opposite direction. The next CEO to be brought in contrasts in every way with the person being displaced. The scene is then set for a swing from one extreme to another.

But there is a third strategy open; which is to take the spotlight off the person for the time being and turn it instead on to how the organization has been operating and where the deficiencies lie. That starting point should precede any decision on who the replacement should be.

A diagnosis of what has gone wrong reveals in many large businesses that the organization is impulsive at the top and slow-moving further down. A further finding usually exposes the failure to use properly the talents that already exist within the organization.

These two typical symptoms of ailing organizations, far from being unrelated are intimately connected. A hierarchy dominated by a single person, who is prone to mistrust others, will ignore the potential of those in the lower ranks to make contributions of value. The price paid for this deliberate oversight will be a queue of things awaiting the personal attention of the boss. All matters requiring decisions are pushed in one direction and the only way in which the growing agenda can then be kept in check is by impetuous decision-making.

I have encountered many examples of impetuosity occurring in such situations. Once an environment has been created conducive to and tolerant of such behaviour at a senior level, necessary preliminary and precautionary measures are given scant consideration. In a corporation renowned for the sophistication of its personnel selection methods, it is all too common to find that a candidate for a senior executive position will be made an attractive job offer by a Mr Big after only the briefest of meetings and on the flimsiest of evidence, often with disastrous consequences.

This should not be dismissed as merely an error of judgement. Rather it is an understandable reaction to the general problem facing a large corporation which is how best to spread the mounting work load in decision-making. One approach is not to spread the work load at all. That is what brings about the crises that follow in the wake of Mr Big.

But if the work load is to be spread, and bearing in mind that complex issues demand more time and attention than simple issues and that a large corporation is likely to be involved in a variety of complex problems all the time, the mechanisms for decision-making have to be constructed.

That aim is not so easy to put into operation. The problem is not technical, nor is it just a matter of finding the people who can make themselves available, for areas that need big decisions should naturally take priority over other claims on attention. The real problem seems to be cultural, even ideological.

Hierarchy works along a one-way vertical channel. The introduction of the concept of horizontality, that is to say of people being involved in parallel management functions at the same level, can scarcely flourish in a system locked into a vertical command structure.

One starting point does exist in that a network of unofficial opinion-making already exists in most corporations. Not that this has anything to do with decision-making. If these unofficial voices were heard by those at the top, they would doubtless be dismissed as uninformed gossip. Yet the reality is that at the middle levels of a corporation there is often no shortage of keen minds nor of people who pride themselves on knowing and commenting on what is going on. Ever ready to guess where certain policies will lead, they can be judged in terms of whether their forecasts are upheld. It happened during my younger consulting days that I was treated by some of these wiseacres as an intimate and was made party to their prognostications. What impressed me was how often well-founded some of their forecasts proved to be.

That discovery posed the problem of whether such potentially useful talents could be brought in to serve a constructive purpose. Many years later I stumbled upon the solution. It was an organizational one, obvious in retrospect but less so in prospect and, as so often, barely imaginable before a particular experience opened the possibilities.

An opportunity to experiment

Crisis creates opportunities. It certainly did for me. The occasion arose when the Chief Executive of a large corporation encountered a stumbling block to his plans for growth and expansion. A man of intellect, drive and ambition, he had reached the conclusion, soon after his appointment, that some of his managers in key positions were not up to the job. He had gone through the painful process of replacing them and had brought in newcomers at very high salaries. Only then did he make the alarming discovery that they too fell short of his expectations. He was now in a jam. To dismiss those newly appointed would have undermined his personal credibility. Conceivably there might be one remaining way forward, which was to find a means of welding them into an effective team.

Using the full range of sophisticated assessment methods we had developed, I was able to secure a complete profile of all the members of his Board and was invited to attend a Board meeting. There were thirteen present. The Chief Executive dominated the meeting which turned out to be as unsatisfactory as meetings of this sort generally are.

Feeling I had nothing to lose, I decided to take a risk. 'I don't think this meeting is going very well', I declared. 'For one thing it is too large. May I suggest that we divide the meeting into two. We can still cover the same agenda.'

So it came about that two groups were set up. With profile information available on all members of the Board, I was granted permission to decide which members should join each of the two groups. Here my aim was to create the best possible team balance. I then appointed two independent persons to observe the two groups as they worked in parallel on a single important problem identified by the Board. At the end of a session of defined length the two groups reconvened and pooled their conclusions. The observers presented their separate reports and the Board members collectively reflected on their experiences.

On all counts this reorganization was hailed an operational success. The smaller groups made for a greater measure of individual participation, the group members combined well and enjoyed the arrangement and each group came up with a range of positive proposals.

The most notable outcome, however, was the variation in the conclusions that each group reached. That was because the groups saw the problem from different angles and therefore were led to create different approaches. These approaches were in some small areas incompatible but in most other respects were complementary. The original problem could now be tackled in greater depth and with greater confidence.

A decision was taken to pursue this organizational strategy further. But then we encountered a sudden reverse. The long-standing and low-profile Chairman of the company retired and a new strong man took his place. In almost no time at all the newcomer and the Chief Executive clashed. The latter left hurriedly and, as happens so often when a new person grabs the reins, all traces of the influence of the original incumbent were removed and the experiment came to an end.

However, this short-lived experiment created some useful learning. When more people are assembled in smaller and parallel groups in place of a single larger group, there is greater value to be gleaned from their deliberations. The only proviso is that a climate needs to be created in which their separate conclusions can be distilled. In a hierarchical organization where all relationships, even between groups, are based on rank, this is not easy to bring about.

If the deployment of concurrent groups is to gain greater acceptance, a case on general grounds needs to be made for its introduction. That case needs to be advocated on the grounds of the desirability of competition. Competition is the watchword of a market economy. Competition in ideas within an organization is just as important as competition between products in the marketplace. There is every reason to believe that the former facilitates success in the latter. Certainly there is a danger of hierarchies becoming monolithic in responding to the challenge of the times. That lack of diversity in thinking provides opportunities for smaller firms, of which there are many, to become one of the main sources of important innovations. But that opportunity is only the obverse of the closing up of opportunities that is the typical feature of the large corporation.

The problem of sequential steps

Groups operating in parallel can furnish a wider range of ideas and innovations than a single large group. But that is not the only advantage of concurrent operation. There are two further advantages that are equally important and generally overlooked.

One major advantage of concurrent teamwork is to shorten the time-span within which demanding matters receive the full attention

The decision-making process

The process by which decisions are reached is of vital importance to how an organization functions and has an added significance according to its interface with team roles. Type 1 represents the sole decision-maker. It is a position in which shapers thrive as leaders. Type 2 is much affected by the team role of the leader but functions especially well where that role is discharged by the co-ordinator. Type 3 is well adapted to an organization that introduces concurrent teams operating competitively. Here the most well-regarded leader often tends to be a monitor evaluator.

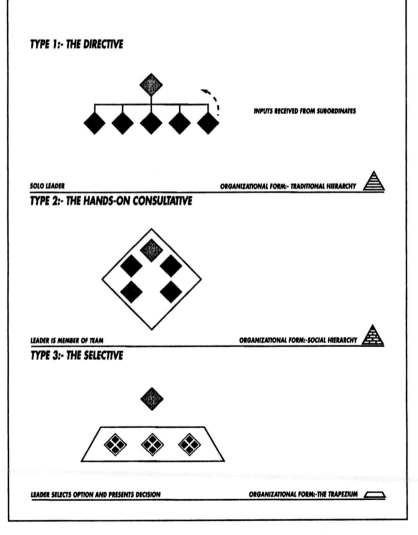

TYPE 1:- THE DIRECTIVE

INPUTS RECEIVED FROM SUBORDINATES

SOLO LEADER · ORGANIZATIONAL FORM:- TRADITIONAL HIERARCHY

TYPE 2:- THE HANDS-ON CONSULTATIVE

LEADER IS MEMBER OF TEAM · ORGANIZATIONAL FORM:-SOCIAL HIERARCHY

TYPE 3:- THE SELECTIVE

LEADER SELECTS OPTION AND PRESENTS DECISION · ORGANIZATIONAL FORM:-THE TRAPEZIUM they deserve. That is made possible because responsibilities are spread. A relatively flat organization geared for concurrent decision-making acts faster than other organizations built for sequential decision-making.

The second advantage attached to concurrent teamwork is that items that fail to make the agenda of management but which rightly should have a place upon it now have a better chance of being considered.

The need here was exposed by a host of examples that came my way during a period when, on behalf of the (then) British Institute of Management, I ran the first courses in the United Kingdom on Total Quality Control. At each seminar I conducted a Quality Calamity exercise. Participants were invited to cite a single instance within their personal experience of one calamity in quality that had cost their company a very large sum of money. They were further asked to estimate what that cost might be and to attribute the prime cause to one of seven prescribed categories.

Over the total period in which I was engaged in running the seminars I collected details on 121 quality calamities. These were often sensational in nature but had been well and truly hidden by firms anxious to retain a favourable public image. Here was one typical example.

A new split-level cooker had been launched on the market under pressure from sales so that there had been no time to carry out the extensive and independent tests which a new product demands. In its first flourish the cooker enjoyed wide popularity, but in the event proved to have one critical defect. The insulation surrounding the oven was inadequate. The build-up of heat which escaped progressively into the controls above was not enough to interfere with their operation during the time cycle of such typical activities as baking a cake. A longer period of continuous heating was needed to reveal the weakness. A large turkey in the oven on Christmas Day provided just such a test, for before the bird was cooked the controls melted. By this time the cookers had been distributed and were in use throughout Great Britain. A lot of people must have had a miserable Christmas dinner!

It would have been nice to reconstruct history to guarantee that nothing would go wrong with the roast turkey. But, leaving aside that reverie, the question to be answered is what do such mishaps show.

Analysis of all 121 calamities in the study revealed that 36 per cent were attributable to what was termed lack of proving, a term covering and including new designs, materials and processes. Another 14 per cent were attributable to the prime cause of poor planning and coordination. Taken together it would seem that failures in field testing, pre-planning and planning itself accounted for half the quality disasters. Each of these calamities could entail a huge financial loss. And while the focus of this study was on quality, it seems likely that a similar study of health and safety disasters would reveal a similar picture, including and in particular, ferry disasters.

The implication seems to be that a great number of unglamorous activities fail to get on to management's agenda because the subject matter is unattractive. People like feedback on their work of a positive and encouraging nature and unfortunately the benefits of avoiding calamities are not visible except in retrospect.

The objection to engaging in more planning and pre-planning is that it slows everything up. That is what happens when all procedures are ordered on the basis of a critical path and are tackled according to some linear sequence. The reaction to what is feared as undue delay is the overhasty response and this is where the disasters come in. By contrast, where organizations are designed to allow for concurrent operations, sounder does not mean slower.

Concurrence and coordination are impossible without teamwork. They are socially difficult to arrange in organizations where people are slotted into highly structured jobs and keep within well defined territories.

Concurrent decision-making and team empowerment

Any sort of decision-making by a team necessitates some degree of team empowerment. In the case of teams operating concurrently there is little sense in making recommendations which then have to be considered afresh by another body of decision-makers. That formula results in fruitless duplication of effort when both bodies arrive at the same conclusions. If the two bodies reach different conclusions, the position is hardly better. The view of the senior body will prevail and the junior body will feel frustrated. What is more, the junior body may have been correct in their diagnosis and recommendations. But there is no way of knowing.

The only sensible basis on which teams can be set up to look at different issues concurrently is by offering them team empowerment. The possession of corporate responsibility allows the overall effectiveness of the team to be assessed. There should be clear criteria by which they will be judged in terms of whether they reach or fail to reach their declared objectives.

In the case of teams set up to look at the same issue in parallel, a different situation arises. Team empowerment is scarcely applicable. The teams are effectively in competition with each other. The aim is the enrichment of outputs rather than responsibility for outcomes. A further process by a third party will still be needed to reconcile the differences in recommendations and to arrive at final decisions.

A challenge to the culture

Given the strong case for developing an organization that can accommodate the work of concurrent teams, questions immediately arise. If the advantage of running concurrent teams in certain situations is real, why does it not happen? Or perhaps, more accurately, why is it so rare? And if the benefit had been established somewhere, would it not have spread rapidly?

The answers to these questions can be no more than hypotheses and speculations. However, it is my belief that this concept of organization is so foreign that it is very difficult to assimilate. Concurrence embodies a spread of power, whereas large organizations are built up around the concept of the centralization of power. In some public bodies the culture revolves around the creation of consensus. But here again there are difficulties.

One key point about concurrence is that, if properly established, it utilizes the strength inherent in the diversity of different teams with their different characteristics within a single umbrella body. It creates competition, excitement and possibly controversy. Yet it remains a managed form of competition. Consensus, on the other hand, discards differences that may lie at the periphery and moves towards common ground. The declaration of differences at some intermediate point would impede the process.

But concurrence is likely to encounter strongest resistance from the champions of hierarchy. True hierarchies depend on the exercise of power. Power is forever on the lookout for potential rivals to itself, as history has demonstrated on so many occasions. It is almost inconceivable that a power-based hierarchy will willingly foster a process that could mount a challenge to its own decision-making supremacy.

The likely explanation of the non-existence of concurrent systems within an organization is that such an innovative introduction would run counter to the ruling culture. Put another way, one might say that a system on these lines would offend the protocol of hierarchy. Such an objection is unlikely to be expressed in exactly those terms. But subconscious resistance is almost certain.

That raises the problem of whether and how hierarchy might evolve into something better adapted to the future. A difficult issue of this nature now deserves careful examination.

6

Replacing traditional hierarchy ——————————

Hierarchy is so ingrained in the nature of organizations of any size that it raises the question of whether humans are capable of working in any other way.

One piece of evidence worth taking into account concerns attitudes to the type of association which people aspire to join. There are many people, especially young people, who opt to work in organizations of a non-hierarchical social character. Communes, cooperatives and partnerships have wide appeal; religious working communities, for whom work is a form of sacrament, are legion; and Israeli kibbutzim attract politically idealistic members from all over the world. There are signs of a strong human wish to belong to an organization in which people can believe, and which they find socially rewarding. The real stumbling-block is that non-hierarchical organizations, however attractive they may be, have difficulty in competing with hierarchical organizations in terms of the normal criteria of business efficiency.

If non-hierarchical organizations are prone to lack competitive advantage, one need not look far to find the points at which their weaknesses are exposed. In their desire to avoid distinctions of rank they shun other forms of distinction between people. Such caution precludes any sophisticated approach to the division of labour. By lacking an efficient means for distributing jobs and responsibilities among their members, non-hierarchical organizations abound with people who are in the wrong jobs or not 'pulling their weight' and are difficult to shift from the positions they occupy. The mechanism for correcting this is undeveloped or even non-existent. It is small wonder that many non-hierarchical bodies are dubbed 'disorganized' in the eyes of their critics.

In contrast, the classic multi-tiered hierarchy suffers from the opposite fault of being 'over-organized'. The price paid for this defect, itself an undue extension of what would otherwise be a virtue, is the emergence of a seemingly mindless and rigid bureaucracy. Given those two extremes, the issue is to find that Golden Path of the middle way.

Drawing the trapezium

At one time I thought I had come near to finding such a path. The formula I had espoused had three key components.

The first was the replacement of multi-tiered hierarchy with a single-stage difference so presenting a two-level managerial model of Organization. The top level embodied strategic management, the second level operational management. Implicit in the design of this model was the rule that strategic managers should not interfere with operational management. The job of strategic managers is primarily to exercise control through resource allocation, including human resource allocation, and general direction-setting. Strategic managers and operational managers are engaged in work that is different in character so that the former are not well placed to supervise the latter in the sense of acting as day-to-day bosses.

The second component followed from the first. If it is impractical for strategic managers to supervise directly the work of operational managers, they need to know intimately what is going on so that strategic management is to make an appropriate contribution to moving or replacing managers at the operational level. Here advances in information technology had made possible what would have been unthinkable a few years ago. Detailed information about the way people contribute and perform, how they operate in teams and how their personal characteristics match the demands made upon them by their jobs is now easily and systematically collected and rapidly relayed. In this context, and following a period of prolonged research in the Industrial Training Research Unit at Cambridge, we had developed Interplace, a human resource management system, soon to become widely used by leading companies around the world. The overall effect of these technical advances was to alter the rules governing the reporting span of accountability. No longer did a corporation need to be bound by the usual notions governing the ratio between senior managers and middle managers, as in a traditional hierarchy. The reporting span under this new arrangement could be doubled, trebled or quadrupled without any loss of crucial information other than that which necessitated personal dialogue.

The third component of the model was a flattening at the top. There is no level in an organization at which teamwork is more important than at the most senior level where matters of great complexity have to be thrashed out. As we saw in Chapter 3, pulling rank kills the free exchange of opinions and ideas. Getting to the right decision on major issues is fraught with problems, but has enormous benefits if it can be accomplished. Here the concept of hierarchy damages dynamic human interaction. The acceptance of teamwork at the philosophic level is a pre-condition for getting the most out of talented managers.

Given these essential components of what I considered an ideal system for managing enterprises and corporations above a certain size, I called the system Trapezium Management. A trapezium is a quadrilateral of which two sides are parallel, in this case the horizontal sides. The other two sides could be sloped at equal acute or even very acute angles according to the view taken on the desired size of the strategic function in relation to the totality of the outfit.

Distorting the trapezium

The introduction of the trapezium model did not have quite the effect I intended. After a while I encountered several managers who alleged that their organizations were operating in exactly that way.

Then it dawned on me that the disadvantage of postulating a trapezium as an organizational model is that its shape is still the familiar pyramid with the minor variant of the truncated apex. Therefore any enterprise with a static structure comprising two levels of management, senior and middle, could claim that it had Trapezium Management already in place. The only further modification of position needed was for senior management to change its title to strategic management and for middle management to be switched to operational management. Apart from these verbal changes the old hierarchical style and system of management could continue much as before.

While I was pondering how to handle this situation, I encountered some arresting cases where large businesses had fallen on hard times as a result of making some calamitous decisions. To give these top managers any credit they deserved, they had at least refrained from interfering with operational management: that they had behaved like strategic managers was beyond doubt. The only criticism was that they were mistaken in their judgements.

Deeper inquiry into the circumstances surrounding this wrong decision-making pointed up revealing instances where a clear contributory cause was that top management (or strategic management) had become detached from operational management. Some operational managers do not think strategically and make no pretence of doing so, but they are close enough to realities to recognize proposals they think will flounder for reasons they can specify. And when what they fear happens, they complain, usually with some justification, that they were never consulted.

The model of Trapezium Management was clearly susceptible to being turned into a two-class system separated by an unbridgeable (or unshiftable) demarcation barrier. That can be the problem when models become structures, for structures are a poor way of representing dynamic processes. I reflected on the way in which the social organization of the higher termites with their ten-foot castles might be represented in terms of an organization chart and reached the conclusion it could not be done.

Division and integration

The division of labour gives a society strength in depth while by the same token erecting barriers to communication. These barriers can be overcome but at a certain cost; for, once the dam is breached, the release of energy generates an untamed flow of its own that threatens to surge forward like a raging torrent that rocks and boulders cannot stop. Therein lies the dilemma: is the strength of an orderly and disciplined division of labour to be maintained, but the dynamism lost; or should the priority be to foster the untamed vitality of the process over all other considerations?

The lesson in organization offered by bees and ants was that its strength lay in its processes. If that lesson was to be taken on board, the trapezium model looked in need of revision. With the benefit of hindsight I recognized my mistake in having conceived managerial work and responsibilities too much in terms of 'jobs'. Certainly there was a case for differentiating between managerial 'jobs' on the grounds that there is strong evidence that managers need different sorts of aptitude in dealing with long-term, middle-term and short-term issues. Some managers demonstrate their abilities in strategic planning, others in coping with urgent operational matters. Solving one problem, that is by making better use of specialization, can have the effect of creating compartmentalism.

There now seemed a case for treating the division of labour issue in another way. The division would focus on processes rather than on personalized jobs. Instead of the job of a leader, a strategic manager and an operational manager one might think instead of a leadership function, a strategic function and an operational function. It is important to make a clear distinction between the terms 'job' and 'function'. The difference is not primarily semantic. In the case of a job, one person is responsible for it; in the case of a function, responsibility is shared by several people. There is here an analogy from sport. One person drops out of a team, but the gap is filled by another and the team performs without having its scoring power diminished. When a group of people act as a team there is always closure whenever a gap occurs. By contrast, when gaps occur in individualized organizations it is never easy for another to take over.

The team in business, industry and the professions can cover any function. By being set up in the right way it will also enjoy functional stability. If the aim is to achieve stability on a broader front, a set of interlocking teams will fulfil the purpose. Whereas the hierarchy of management is nearly always represented in terms of jobs, the preferred alternative in the years ahead is likely to be a hierarchy of teams.

The significance of this newer model is that lower levels (in salary and seniority terms) are not necessarily shut out from higher functions. A strategic team may be in a better position to reach its objectives if it includes an appropriate person at the current operating level. As in sport no one has a right to an automatic place in a team. Places have to be earned.

Team-based hierarchies are not subject to the rigidities associated with personalized hierarchies because there are no individual territories to defend. A fuller treatment of the prospects of this type of organization will be given in Chapter 14.

Model, culture or person? Which comes first?

It is my contention that the surest way of replacing the rigidities of bureaucracy with the spirit of enterprise is to transfer power to the team that has to deal with a given span of responsibility. When mismanaged companies fail, the underlying weakness of Organization is seldom the issue brought to light. Nearly always the problem is personalized. Heads roll and whoever is nearest the helm is the first to the chopping block.

But times are changing. It is no longer as predictable as it used to be that a new Mr Big will be sought to replace the old Mr Big. Searches are starting to be made for an able Chief Executive with personal characteristics to match the culture of the corporation. These new forays into the making of appointments are restricted by the difficulties corporations find in defining their own culture. The attempt to do so inevitably raises the question: is this what the corporation is really like, or is this what the corporation is trying to be?

Defining the current culture is a passive way of attempting to kindle organizational vitality. The shape of Organization plays its own peculiar part in imposing a certain kind of culture. And if a new shape is being planned it is inevitable that it will have cultural implications. Models deal with different types of shape; moreover, they invite choice.

If the starting model is one of the design of Organization, the next step will be the choice of the leading players to fit that model. The culture that is developed will then be an outgrowth of that model. If one starts with a Chief Executive, a personalized stamp will be placed on the total corporation or enterprise and the culture that springs from

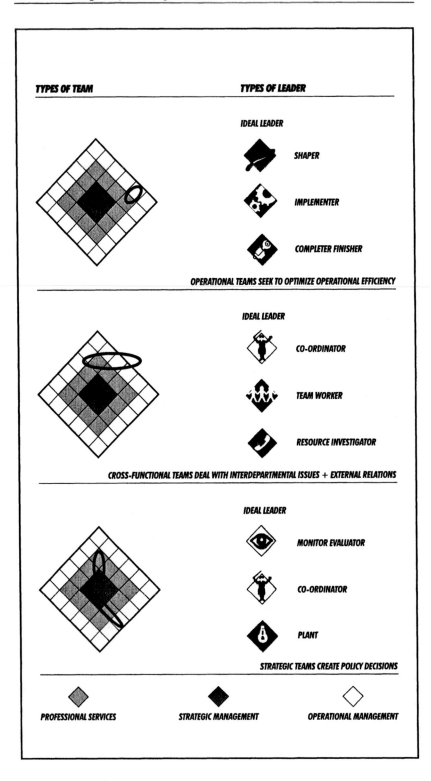

TYPES OF TEAM

TYPES OF LEADER

IDEAL LEADER

SHAPER

IMPLEMENTER

COMPLETER FINISHER

OPERATIONAL TEAMS SEEK TO OPTIMIZE OPERATIONAL EFFICIENCY

IDEAL LEADER

CO-ORDINATOR

TEAM WORKER

RESOURCE INVESTIGATOR

CROSS-FUNCTIONAL TEAMS DEAL WITH INTERDEPARTMENTAL ISSUES + EXTERNAL RELATIONS

IDEAL LEADER

MONITOR EVALUATOR

CO-ORDINATOR

PLANT

STRATEGIC TEAMS CREATE POLICY DECISIONS

PROFESSIONAL SERVICES   STRATEGIC MANAGEMENT   OPERATIONAL MANAGEMENT

The positioning of teams within the organization

The traditional top-down chart of the hierarchical organization has lost its relevance to modern conditions. Instead, the positioning of managers in relation to one another can be represented as if in a different location on a chequerboard. Each manager will have a particular orbit of operations but these operations are interdependent and often of equal importance.

Teams are of three types. *Operational teams* are usually internal to a department or business function, while providing room for an external professional. It is no disadvantage if they are managed in a semi-hierarchical style. *Cross-functional teams* cannot be handled as if part of a hierarchy, for they involve co-ordination between departments or functions of equal standing: in some cases they involve customers and clients external to the boundaries of the firm. *Strategic teams*, rather than comprising solely strategic members, should always incorporate operational managers and professional services to provide the necessary balance but the presence of a single strategic manager serves to empower the team for the decisions it reaches. Due to the slower pace of strategic teams, concurrence is an essential requirement if an organization is to maintain a wide grip on its overall affairs.

Leadership involves different personal aptitudes in each of these three teams. Experience with team-role technology suggests the ideal pattern as shown on the chart opposite.

it will last only so long as that particular person stays in office. If the starting point is culture and activities are fashioned to make them compatible with that culture, it may be difficult to establish whether change is real or superficial and short-lived.

The point of human Organization is to create an effective formula for getting work done. So how one approaches the definition and description of a job is very much a basic issue.

7

An alternative way
of arranging work ──────────

The standard human way of organizing work for others is for a senior to decide what work needs to be done, to establish how it should be done and then to get someone to do it. The whole process can operate with commendable efficiency under conditions of stability. But once conditions change, the system is liable to be thrown into disarray.

That piece of learning occurred at an early stage of my industrial career, although it was only in retrospect some years later that the lessons really registered. The occasion arose when I was asked to help a small engineering company specializing in lithographic printing on metal and in producing a range of associated fabrications. The position, as it was explained to me, was that there was a very strong demand for printed trays: a middleman was keen to buy all that the factory could produce. The problem was that the factory was unable to meet its target outputs.

Having received some training in industrial engineering, I duly set about rationalizing the production process, an activity which included setting an output bonus for the press-operators making the trays. All went well for two weeks. Then I received a call from an indignant Managing Director. So great had been the increase in productivity that the customer was obliged to call a temporary halt to purchases. As a result, the factory girls were sitting round in idleness and complaining vociferously about the loss of their bonus-related take-home pay.

The press-operators had been engaged on tasks of very short duration which allowed for little or no discretion on their part. It was hardly to be expected that they would show discretion when the work ran out. Any display of initiative would have been out of line with the fundamental way in which repetitive work is organized. The more closely jobs are specified by a third party, the harder it becomes for workers to adjust their behaviour in an appropriate way when conditions change. They are not brought into confidence on the overall production schedules of the company and of the way in which the fluctuating market can affect demand for the different items.

After the last war an industrial climate was created which placed a great emphasis on production volumes. That was because almost anything that could be produced could be sold. Individual incentives became the order of the day. But soon the disadvantages began to outweigh the advantages. As the market became more discriminating, production runs became shorter. With a growing need for more adaptable workers, who could cope with variations in production runs, the continued existence of individual incentive schemes was found to be detrimental to versatility in the labour force.

The emphasis now swung from incentive schemes to job specifications. Whereas incentive schemes were built on closely studied tasks, job specifications encompassed a compilation of duties without the detail being spelled out on how those duties were to be discharged. Whatever the original attention may have been, the effect of the job specification was to exercise a major effect on the social nature of work.

A mechanism for undermining teamwork

It is normal practice for anyone starting a new job to be given a job description defining the work to be undertaken in general terms. However, in some corporations the generality of job descriptions fell short of the demands of the bureaucracy. Individuals working alongside one another often need to know who does what, and the corporation likes to know also. There are only two ways of sorting that out. Either adjacent workers have to decide among themselves or a third party, in a managerial position, intervenes to make the decision for them. The creation of a job specification served to eliminate any confusion before it could arise.

A clearer definition of the boundaries of those working in close proximity was supposed to be one of the advantages of the job specification. But frontiers also have a divisive effect. Someone who 'poaches' on the work on another, or in other words crosses the frontier, is in the vulnerable position of being an intruder. It is safer to stay on one's own patch. If everyone adheres to their own defined set of duties, the system should work. Or rather, the system would work given an ideal set of conditions. These conditions require the needs for interaction between the jobs to be fully understood in the first instance and thereafter for continued stability in balance between the jobs, with the latter depending on the stable nature of demands from the external world.

It was my experience that these two conditions were very seldom met. Production always seems to be in a state of flux. What usually happened was that once departments of corporations had published job specifications for all the jobs, the resultant material would soon be found obsolete. The management would therefore have the choice either of revising the job specifications or leaving them as they were and creating another job in order to embrace the new work content.

Faced with this unattractive dilemma, the management often did neither. They were then placed in a difficult position. Expressed colloquially, it meant saying:

> Yes, I know we've just completed your job specifications but we would be grateful if you could do some additional work. No, we can't offer additional payment for these extra duties. After all, some of these new duties will replace those you normally undertake. That is arguable, you say. Well, we will review the job specification as soon as we find the time, but meanwhile . . .

Often the additional, and less task-related, duties not covered in the job specification involved some form of liaison work. This would be unconsciously resented or even consciously resisted because it was seen as an unpaid imposition. Nor was it just a matter of the money. Individual job specifications tended to consolidate boundaries between jobs, thereby creating demarcation barriers that impeded cooperative behaviour and teamwork.

Given this difficult situation, management took the easy way out. Extra jobs were created to cover the new work content revealed once all the job specifications were complete. That is why so many corporations, engaged in introducing widespread programmes of job specification, paid with overmanning for their indulgences and lack of foresight.

Empowering the team and managing its consequences

The weakness of employing bodies of any size is typically that responsibility falls between stools. If anything goes wrong, it is usually the fault of someone else or another department. The fragmentation of responsibility and the confinement of people within the rigid limits of their own specific jobs means that problems are never seen as a whole. Complaints are seldom properly resolved. During a period of personal involvement with issues of quality in industry, I encountered a recurring phenomenon. A faulty item would be returned to the factory and a replacement would be sent with a courteous note of apology. The snag was that the replacement item often contained exactly the same fault as the item being returned. It was never anybody's business to tackle prevention because that could have involved crossing job boundaries.

Individual responsibility offers a much lower level of service than team responsibility. Individuals may argue about who exactly is responsible for what, whereas a team is responsible for the result. How any problem arising is best resolved then becomes an internal matter.

Team empowerment offers a new means of organizing work at a local level. The focus now shifts from the tasks to the output that is needed. It is up to the team to produce the results, which means that the members of the team have to divide the work in the most appropriate way between themselves. Team empowerment only works if the team is given the resources by management. Resources mean money, machines and people. How the three are best combined is up to the team.

It is difficult for team empowerment to work unless management relinquishes insistence on control over the process. That is why team empowerment fits so uncomfortably in a system of traditional hierarchy. But once that close control is lifted, various things follow. The first is that a payment system needs to be changed to reflect team performance rather than individual seniority. The second consequence is that the team develops a keen interest in having the right people in the team. Shirkers and misfits are not tolerated. Here there is a contrast with the position in traditional hierarchies where workers gang up against management when the job of an individual worker is threatened. A threat to one is a threat to all, for all see themselves in possession of similar individual contracts.

Team empowerment generates a need to foster team education. The members need to know what constitutes a good team; they need to know how to combine to best effect, how to improve the balance of the team, what sort of people to look for and how to trade in people. But here trading is not about buying and selling but about career development; this will be considered in the next chapter.

Another feature of team empowerment is that members have to cover for one another in the case of temporary absence. This need brings about a modified form of career development within the team. Rotating between jobs within a team is personally fulfilling for certain types of personality. That in turn bears on the social attributes that denote the good team member and may override the sort of merit that is based solely on technical competence.

Moving people around within the organization is a good way of discovering latent talents. Sometimes these talents can be identified and developed and serve to provide candidates for jobs that would otherwise be hard to fill. We tried to underline the importance of this subject by sponsoring an industrial film, made by Video Arts, called *Selecting The Perfect Team*. In this film a candidate with the 'ideal' qualifications turns out to be a disaster, while a promising candidate in the work group whose skills have not been fully developed was overlooked. As the story develops, it transpires that the solving of a career problem and the solving of a vacancy problem can be overcome by revising the strategy of making appointments.

Creating a more broad-based form of work

When people work together, the business on which they are engaged is more than an aggregate of separate tasks. Yet in some institutions, especially those in the public domain, it is the task that occupies the prime focus of attention and activity. Professionalism is about professional tasks which are undertaken without due account being taken of other considerations.

The two conspicuous examples occur in the fields of education and health. Expressed in task terms, the job of the teacher is to dispense knowledge, that is part of an agreed curriculum, to pupils. The job of the nurse is to administer to patients a set of pre-learned nursing services; the job of the doctor is to prescribe an appropriate set of medicines to ill people. If these professionals confine themselves to their technical competencies, the school and the hospital will run into a conflict of priorities that centre on the difference between the needs and expectations of 'clients' and the notions of professionals about what their job comprises.

Consider education in the first place. Education, the saying goes, is what is left when you have forgotten what you have learned. The 'clients' of education expect to grow and develop personally, to be able to think for and to teach themselves in meeting the challenges of the external world. Those who make it happen, who imbue their pupils with a love of a subject and a desire to go on learning are readily identified and recognized as 'great teachers' by a consensus in the neighbourhood community. In contrast, the school or college itself is not officially aware of its true educators and makes no serious attempt to find out. It would be easy to do so and to publicize the result in the same way that a hotel finds a way of highlighting the 'employee of the month' by asking clients for nominations. That simple procedure would be to offend the rules of protocol in the typical institution.

There are two further outputs of education, peripheral perhaps to its central purpose, but important to the community at large. One relates to the ability of the school to turn out law-abiding citizens who show respect for other members of the community. The converse of this is shown in figures on juvenile delinquency. Strong attempts were made by the educational establishment to suppress such figures as they relate to differences between schools, which can be notable and therefore offer significant lessons. These lessons are unlikely to be learned, when the view is that crime is a subject best handled by another department of society. Here teachers are in a cleft stick. The school is not wholly accountable for the discipline of its pupils to its local client population nor for answering for the means by which it is enforced. The rules governing punishment are set by outside bodies beyond the locality and kept in place by the ever-present threat of the law. Legal sanctions can be taken capriciously against teachers and the education authority, even where acting within a framework agreed collectively by parents and governors.

Disturbed children constitute another category to which the school may be expected to make some response. The problem this presents falls outside the core tasks for which teachers are trained. Again, the problem is side-stepped by passing it over to some outside body.

The increase in the range of pressures now being placed on schools is nowhere more strongly felt than in the state of the school budget. The introduction of local financial management, which is perhaps the first ray of light in the devolution of management in education, has meant that the school has been obliged to react in some positive way. The first reaction was of rejection: teachers could not be expected to become business people. But, in due course, the school began to adapt. The means of adjusting was by discovering latent skills and aptitudes of teachers that could be utilized in this context. Education has begun to discover for itself the meaning of teamwork and of extending the range of its potential contribution to society, given the lifting of hierarchy and the prospect of increasing the resources needed for operating in a broader framework.

In the field of health the division of labour is primarily organized round tasks which have a more set pattern about them than those in education. A nurse in hospital will commonly wake a patient in the routine of bed-making in order to make the bed more comfortable for the sleeping patient. A consultant's rounds will fall on a particular day even though for some patients this will mean that beds may be occupied for two or so days more than the medical need would justify. The division of labour is so ritualized in terms of tasks that the devolution of responsibility is precluded in an absolute sense. The ward sister (or manager, to use the exaggerated term now preferred) does not possess the powers to discharge the patient even when progress fully meets the criteria that the consultant has laid down. Two instances of the rulebook were considered so scandalous that they made national headline news. In one instance an experienced theatre nurse extracted an appendix in the presence of a surgeon. Both were suspended from duty pending disciplinary proceedings. In another instance an experienced ward sister signed a note for medicines in lieu of, and with the knowledge of, the doctor. Once again, it became a matter of national outrage. In neither of these instances did the breach of rules create any problem for the patient.

The current situation is that team empowerment is an attractive mode of working in the world of education and health since many professionals operate at the same status level and wish to associate with one another as equals. The difficulty arises in so far as the institutional hierarchy is backed by the regulatory bodies of government and its insistence on taking up a super-managerial role. To trust teachers and health workers would be to claw back power from a central authority. Yet the extra pressures loaded on to professionals require them to enlarge their areas of responsibility. Only by finding new ways of working together in coping with that responsibility can they hope to succeed. The paradox is that they are encased in a culture brimful of barriers for those wishing to journey far down that chosen road.

Differentiating between structured and unstructured work

Whatever the background against which work has to be carried out, some means has to be found for assigning work to members of a workforce. In principle there are two prime methods. One is for a boss, or the technical assistants of a boss, to prescribe the tasks to be performed along with the method of operation and the quality standards to be met. Structured work is especially favoured by hierarchical systems. The second type of work is unstructured: that is to say it is of a more variable nature and is subject to a more uneven flow. Here the ability to cope with the work efficiently demands flexibility and cooperation between a group of people charged with a broad measure of responsibility.

In any single enterprise of any size, whether in the public or private sector, structured and unstructured work will coexist. The mistake, so easily made, is to fail to recognize that fact. Work may be treated as structured when far better results could be achieved if it were unstructured and managed as such. Conversely, there are some operations where the observance of certain standards, as in the case of safety, is critical and to treat this work as unstructured would be a grave mistake.

A possible and much favoured division of labour is to channel some members of the labour force into structured work and others into unstructured work, so producing, in effect, a separation between those committed to routine drudgery and the rest. That is scarcely a pattern that appeals or can continue to appeal in a liberal and educated society. The other approach is to recognize that for most people both types of work have to be incorporated in a job. In other words, there exists a core of specified, routine tasks that need to be undertaken, while beyond that core lies a body of variable work that is no less important and may even be more important. This work beyond the core can only be settled in conjunction with others and by recognition of the needs of the immediate situation.

The form of Organization that belongs to this second pattern is already well established. It flourishes in the world of bees and ants. But it has yet to establish itself in human society, for organic to our world is the notion that all Organization is based on hierarchy. Work is an involuntary activity which will not be undertaken without the exercise of power by someone. In so far as that is what people believe, work will always be distasteful. It will also be conducted inefficiently, for it will be unable to match the level of adaptability of worker bees and worker ants in their respective forms of corporate working behaviour.

I hear a contention that people will never behave like worker bees and worker ants because it is not in their nature. That is a credible proposition. Yet it must also be borne in mind that work can spring from human nature. We see it in the case of individuals reputed to be workaholics or in the case of communities of workers who identify with their industry and feel fulfilled and uplifted by what they are doing.

It is clear that work is not a homogeneous activity but has many aspects including the way in which it is set up by the manager. A particular configuration of work will suit some people but not others. Hence the need for a strategy to mediate between the needs to get things done and to distribute work in the best possible way between any given group of workers. Developments in this field are proceeding and are further referred to in the Appendix.

8

Teams communicate with teams ————————————

To travel beyond the world of structured work with its core tasks is to enter a realm occupied primarily by people engaged in activities that they settle between them. Whether that formula justifies itself or not in practice depends on a great number of factors. A team that achieves success, whose members adapt to each other and work well together, deserves to continue as it is. And that will normally happen. Further, if success can be maintained even under varying conditions and demands, it will provide testimony to the team's good internal balance and to its capacity for regulating itself through shared insights. In that way it can draw on its various parts for different strengths at different times. That is the ideal. However, the ideal is not the rule. What usually happens is that a run of good fortune is followed by a series of reverses or a long period of stagnation. The set-back then poses the question as to what so unexpectedly can have gone wrong.

In my previous book, *Team Roles At Work*, I described this phenomenon as I had encountered it in connection with long-term research and development projects. The explanation, according to my interpretation, was that a project goes through stages, each of which has a critical focus. As a rule, I found there were six stages. The first involved the identification of needs and objectives; the second, the creation of ideas that pointed the way forward; the third, the formulation of plans based on a considered choice between competing options; the fourth, the making of contacts, for nothing ever works unless it wins the support of others; the fifth, the setting up of an organization involving both the definition of working practices and the assignment of people to those duties; and the sixth, follow through, for anything that can go wrong is likely to reveal itself at the earliest stages.

Diagnosis of and inquest on team failures in a number of instances brought out the tendency for problems to occur with particular players in the team at particular stages. Key individuals would carry their distinctive contribution at one stage over into the next for which it was inappropriate. Sometimes the only way in which that person could be prevented from holding up progress was by ejection from the team. I came across several sad instances of highly inventive scientists being removed from a team in order to facilitate the commercial launch of a product, and of founders of companies being dismissed from a Board to enable the company to move into a bigger commercial league. Yesterday's heroes can become today's obstacles.

The dismissal of a player from a team that has previously been working well is a demoralizing business. The chances of needing to take such a step can be minimized by educating the team in team-role theory and in related practical exercises. By that means, the members learn to appreciate how they best function in combination and how each can best contribute to the whole.

Given ideal handling of a delicate situation, problems in this area can be avoided or reduced. But this is not an ideal world. There comes a moment in the life of a team or working group where there is general recognition that a team member would be better placed elsewhere. It happens in football and often leads to huge transfer fees. In the world of business and industry the mechanisms for bringing about a change of team personnel are more rudimentary and often agonizing. A team member whose heyday has passed can apply for a job in another company, while taking special care to hide what can be interpreted as an act of disloyalty from other members of the firm; or can wait nervously for the axe to fall.

Changing team as part of a career development plan

Satisfaction at work has a great deal to do with meeting expectations. If an individual expects to stay in a winning team, it is a great disappointment to be removed. The surest safeguard against disappointment and disillusion is a better management of expectations.

There can hardly have been a more opportune time to bring about a change in people's career expectations than the present. The delayering of organizations has already undermined the hopes of employees that the reward for correct and virtuous behaviour would be eventual promotion. The steps on the upward ladder have been sawn off and straightforward climbing has been made more and more difficult. Those whose careers hold out more promise are those who are imputed to have more versatility. They are people who, in a sense, have a facility for jumping between ladders.

In flat organizations lateral career development now presents the most feasible option for the majority of employees. But here a word of caution has to be expressed, for feasibility does not denote advisability. It is not advisable for a person to move from a suitable position to an unsuitable one; on the other hand, it is very advisable to move from an unsuitable position to a more suitable one. So how does the feasible get translated into the advisable?

It is my contention that it is in the interests of everybody to establish what it is that a person does best and to steer that person towards the area where that strength has an appropriate outlet. The rider of this proposition is that a person's work associates are the best judges of what a person most contributes at work. Once a person's work contribution is expressed in a transferable language, which is meaningful in different situations, it can be related to an array of work demands. It is then easy in theory to establish where a person is best placed.

The technology for making this happen has been the centrepiece of our research and development work for a number of years and in Interplace we produced an expert system now widely used for this very purpose. The sub-systems of the software program protected the main program against poor assessors and have been designed to extract the most meaningful information from a range of inputs.

The result of this technological advance was that a person who had become redundant in meeting needs at a particular stage in a project could be nominated within seconds for another more suitable job in another position or another team. All that was necessary was to resort to the search programme on the job bank. The existence of the job did not mean that it was available. Switching people between jobs and teams within a firm is a complex political process. But psychologically it made it much easier to extract someone from a team if there was at least the prospect of moving into another position. It would be nice to introduce a new ethical guideline: no-one should be dismissed from a position without being offered another in exchange.

A policy of continuous deployment would constitute a positive step in the right direction. The message to be proclaimed is that no employee has a permanent hold on any particular job but is offered instead a career; or, if not a full career since the number of jobs depends on external factors, then career assistance. Planned movement between positions is part of the career plan.

Enter the Casting Director

Such a policy needs someone to orchestrate it. In *Team Roles At Work* I underlined the need for firms to appoint a Casting Director. It is a responsibility that could be taken up by either a Line Manager or a

Human Resources Director. In a way it does not matter who takes it on as long as the person possesses the necessary skills.

I have not changed my mind since making the original recommendation. If anything, intervening experiences have reinforced the importance of creating such a position. People can stay too long in a particular job and, when they become dissatisfied or are seen by others to be ineffective, they detract from the achievement of goals to which the group is working. Those who are not contributors become passengers.

To move individuals out of a team into another position, once the stage of that person's particular contribution has past, demands three conditions.

The first is that career development, along with planned movement between jobs and teams, is promoted as the cornerstone of employment policy. The need here is to extend beyond mere announcement to an internal educational programme which invites active participation.

The second is that continuous assessment provides the database which is used in a positive way to get the right person into the right job in the right team at the right time. Everybody contributes to the provision of that information. The computer-based technical systems for making this happen are already in place in many corporations, even though the political support systems and the political will to get it working may be lacking.

The third provision is that a Casting Director is charged with facilitating the process. The computer storage of the information means that it is quite feasible to generate within seconds a next job possibility for every employee. The Casting Director will then work with others on the political and training side to see whether what is feasible can be made actual.

These conditions create a new environment within which team empowerment can operate. If teams are given responsibilities which they achieve and are rewarded financially, and moreover are not rewarded when they fail to reach their objectives, teams soon become very interested in maintaining the highest level of team effectiveness. The idea of losing a member as part of an exchange for another begins to become acceptable, provided it is not felt to be operating to the detriment of anyone.

In the absence of the sum total of these conditions, teams are usually difficult to modify with complete consent, for a certain loyalty develops between team members even if they are achieving little. If people feel that transfer between teams presents new opportunities and challenges, the whole thing becomes exciting.

Unfortunately there is a fairly small margin between what excites and what arouses suspicion. That is why the role of the Casting Director is so critical in allaying fears and selling the positive benefits. The mood of the team as a whole, however, will set the tone as to whether continuous development, with forays into other areas, or intended incremental improvement becomes the order of the day and whether the Casting Director is listened to.

I have experimented with these conditions in the context of management games on senior management courses and the willingness to explore new possibilities seems to depend on the creation of a jolly atmosphere. The facilitating role of the Casting Director is more easily recognized in an established firm than on a training course, because a personal reputation can be built up over a longer period than in the former where experiences are usually of short duration. In the case of the sandwich course, the facilitating opportunities are greater because personal reputations can be built up over longer periods.

What I have found is that once a few successful instances of 'personnel swapping' have been experienced, there is no turning back. Individuals and teams expect people to move on to positions where their contribution can be made to better effect with or without a Casting Director. Teams are now starting to use the database on their own account, for it does not need a hierarchy to make it happen.

Teams create a marketplace for their renewal

That is as far as we have got. Things are only beginning to happen in this direction, for it is only recently that information technology, as it applies to the use of human resources, has become widely available at the operating level. Teams are now reaching the stage where they say: 'We must have a Completer'. Another common declaration is: 'We are in need of a good Coordinator.' There are people with special behavioural shapes who are required for particular positions and teams have started to search for them.

Nevertheless, a more general problem has arisen about career development that needs to be mulled over. Internal career development within the corporation contains an element of push and pull. Experience shows that some individuals are wanted in various positions by several people: the pull factor is operating to their favour. There are others who are readily placed on the transfer list: that is the push factor operating against them. In effect there is a marketplace, to which the readier use of information technology gives an added emphasis. The push and pull factors soon translate into supply and demand. And since economists tell us that supply and demand govern prices, a mechanism exists for determining salary progression.

To use that information as a basis of salary progression, or as a means of halting such progression, becomes a controversial matter. Economics tells us it should be used, although popularity, as measured by demand, may be too narrow a way of looking at a person's effectiveness.

Yet one feels the information is too important to be ignored. The advantage of tying it up with the 'price' of labour is that it modifies demand for a commodity in rare supply. By placing people in a price band the demand for their services can be restricted if the labour and professional services needed by a work group is taken and charged as part of the cost. People in greater demand would be more costly, so, according to economic principles, with the price increasing, demand would fall.

Usually information on the 'person overheads' of operations is ignored. That is why one finds meetings with sometimes twelve or more people present that drag on and on. The squandering of such human resources is permitted because it is an unmeasured cost. It is therefore 'free'. If it were measured, and treated as no more than a notional charge, it would be another matter.

The more general point is that information technology, coupled with the human relations skills that go with it, can provide a quantitative measure of a person's most characteristic contributions at work, in team-role terms, and is already playing its part in some large corporations. The information can be readily summoned at a moment's notice, although the identity of the person may be coded and its release is governed by political considerations. This can be a delicate matter because the input material involves what is called 'three hundred and sixty degree assessment'. That somewhat geometric description relates to a process whereby everybody assesses everybody else with whom they have a close personal relationship, irrespective of rank. Apprehension about the effect of prejudice or blandness is offset by the ability of the computer sub-system to recognize bias or undiscriminating perception. With such inputs being filtered out, the overall integrity and reliability of the system is protected.

In principle a means is developing for teams to control their own intake and to improve their balance in order to meet the ever-changing requirements being placed upon them.

Teams assist in career development

It is impolitic for a team to attempt to replace a member without providing assistance for the one who leaves. The ideal way in the program we developed and are using is to operate the search for the job most compatible with a given person-shape. Some personnel exchanges in the replacement field can work out to mutual advantage.

However, such a happy outcome cannot be counted on. The more usual situation is that someone who, in effect, is being ousted cannot immediately find another suitable position. We have learned that some individuals fit into very particular niches. They may spend some time moving from position to position until suddenly they find the right spot. There they perform well and are happy and there they stay. Clearly, the combination of interest in the job, ability to meet its various demands, and to relate to close associates at work, is such a complex matter that the best that can be offered is an opportunity or a series of opportunities in an area of possibility. The less a person has settled down and is in a growing phase, the more relevant this strategy becomes.

That raises the question of how far teams can usefully communicate with teams in other establishments. The aim is not to operate as an employment agency, with all the complexities that have to be handled, but to offer a development and learning opportunity. The precedent here is the model originated by Reg Revans with his Learning Company (Garrett, B., *Creating the Culture of the Learning Organization*; see Further Reading). The idea behind this system of practical management education is that executives learn by being lent to other companies in a series of exchange assignments. It is a proposition especially suited to meeting the needs of an up-and-coming person of recognized potential whose career to date has been confined to a single establishment.

Such an initiative can be sponsored by teams because as they become increasingly empowered so should their responsibilities grow in looking after their members.

Robust teams create pressures on organizations

The ability of teams to steer themselves, to bring in the people they want and to assist their old boys and old girls in their forward careers is a feature of teams that have reached a very advanced stage in their development. That advance, however, has ramifications that can threaten the very heart and soul of contemporary organizations. That is why any movement in this direction risks being spotted and aborted on the grounds that it could undermine the functions of management at the central level.

The present position is that technology is offering social responsibilities to teams that are bound to impact on the current nature of Organization. In the short term the links are more likely to disturb existing systems than to improve them, for they pose something of a dilemma.

In a bureaucracy responsibilities are so clearly set out and sharply defined that rigidity sets in. Should the rigidity be loosened, it is not progress that follows but uncertainty. The team and the hierarchy all too easily face some prospective overlap in their responsibilities and the seeds of conflict are sown for the ownership of territory. Alternatively, recognition of the danger can lead to avoidance behaviour by both parties.

My experience is that the latter is the more likely consequence. People have other priorities to which they must attend. When faced with a choice between the controversial and the uncontroversial, they stick to the safer option. The general subject of improving the balance of the team, which I contend should be the responsibility of the team itself, and of developing the careers of team members once they have served their time with the team, is ignored. Hence important matters fail to register themselves within the accepted terms of reference of either the team or the hierarchy.

Nevertheless, the subject remains latent, for lack of attention does not mean it has disappeared. As bureaucracy is weakened and loses some of its grip, the powers and responsibilities of the team advance. Teams now require a form of organization that will allow them to look after their own interests and those of their members.

9
Employing the highly talented —

Most businesses and public bodies need some measure of above-average talent if they are to progress and then to retain any pre-eminence they may have achieved. The problem, however, is that in all areas of human endeavour high-order human talent is scarce, while at the same time it has to be accepted that standard approaches based on average people seldom deliver excellence. As a result, a choice often has to be made in practice between employing a broad band of above-average talent in adequate supply or a very small amount of exceptional talent in rare supply. Throughout the arts, and especially in music, exceptional talent counts: it is the truly gifted artist who draws the crowds rather than the competent. In the very different field of business, lone entrepreneurs with flair have an impressive record of setting up innovative industries and surpassing the efforts of much larger competitors.

In the field of science, the position is much the same. Jewkes and co-workers in *The Sources of Invention* (see Further Reading) have subjected to close study the seventy inventions judged to have done most to transform everyday life in the twentieth century. They reach the following verdict:

> More than one-half of the cases can be ranked as individual inventions in the sense that much of the pioneering work was carried through by men who were working on their own behalf without the backing of research institutions, and usually with limited resources and assistance; or, where inventors were employed in institutions, these institutions were, as in the case of universities, of such a kind that the individuals were autonomous, free to follow their own ideas without hindrance.

Jewkes' list of the many things we take for granted includes air conditioning, the ball-point pen, domestic gas refrigeration, penicillin, power steering, quick freezing, the radio and the zip fastener.

A typical story of how an invention has preceded a product is exemplified in the case of two young classical musicians. In each hotel they occupied while on tour they ensured that they were given a room with a good bathroom suite, in which they could carry out their experiments on their hobby – colour photography. Their groundwork laid the basis for the successful Kodachrome process, an area in which the well-equipped Kodak laboratories had been striving over years for the awaited breakthrough.

There are many similar person-based stories that lie behind industrial inventions or major projects that have transformed an environment. Two came my way while working in Australia. The economy of the Northern Territory was transformed by an engineer who devised the 'mad' scheme of bringing electricity to Darwin all the way from Alice Springs, a distance of 1200 kilometres. For many years he had no real supporters. But he pressed ahead with his vision and plans until he finally won through. Another case was when Western Australia was afflicted by an almost permanent water shortage for most of the months of the year until a Scottish engineer devised and put into operation a major hydro-electric scheme in the face of unrelenting opposition and scepticism. Just before the project went on stream, fearing a humiliating failure, he committed suicide. Had he lived a little longer he would have witnessed his project being acclaimed an outstanding success.

Back in the UK, I used to work in a major rubber group which had a large research centre. The most successful tyre the group ever produced, however, came not from the research centre but from a discussion in the canteen between a sales executive and a production engineer. Another experience that came my way related to a research worker with asthma. Working on a drug to relieve asthma, he short-circuited the usual testing procedures by trying things out on himself. The pharmaceutical company that employed him made an enormous amount of money. Some of that was invested in new multistorey research laboratory. But the new laboratory never produced a product as cost-effective as that of the research worker with asthma.

These instances pose an issue no that student of Organization can ignore: where should the emphasis lie, on the individual or the team?

The posing of such a question introduces, of course, a false antithesis. A well-designed organization, with a capacity for using its human resources to advantage, should be capable of utilizing the talents of individual genius, if it can be located and harnessed, along with that of the creative team. Both enrich the vitality of the enterprise. In reality, however, the preference will always be for the services of the team.

While it is almost axiomatic that talented people dislike highly structured organizations, perhaps less well known, but equally true, is the converse proposition. Highly structured organizations do not, in the light of my experience, care for highly talented individuals. It is not exactly the talent to which they object, but the behaviour that goes with the talent.

I have spent a fair amount of my time helping companies to cope with talented people who are judged to be misfits. The problem boils down to this: talented people like to create their own structures, to operate within terms of reference that they have helped to create. They wince when presented with standard conditions of employment. To fit into an organization is a betrayal of personal identity. They delight in breaking the rules. They criticize those for whom they would be expected to show respect. They love to operate in an environment with the minimum of constraints. In short, they are virtually unemployable in a conventional organization. Some organizations set out to recruit high-level talent in the belief that that is what they need. The disappointing outcome is often a persistent exodus of talent.

There are certain talented people who are aware that they are not easy to employ and who can sometimes be counselled to good effect. The best advice is to encourage them to exercise their talent as best they can, wherever the opportunity presents itself, but in all other contexts to engage in very orthodox behaviour. In that way they improve their prospects of becoming acceptable employees.

Loosening up the organization

It would be an exaggeration, however, to suggest that the main problem presented by very gifted employees lies in managing their personal idiosyncrasies. The major issue is the inability of the organization to adapt itself to the gifted individual.

In Chapter 7 a case was made for a more elastic way of setting up the job, involving a separation between structured and unstructured work, between work precisely specified for the individual to perform and discretionary work which is shared with others. The gifted individual, in possession of business flair, may not fit too well into either part of this format. Nor will certain types of creative scientist.

Here one has a case of the mountain and Mohammed. If the mountain won't go to Mohammed, Mohammed must go to the mountain. The variant is that if the individual cannot be tailored to the work, the work must be tailored to the individual. From the perspective of the employer the mountain in this case is the individual rather than the work. Coping with some individuals can be like attempting to climb a difficult mountain. One needs a mountain guide. In real life these mountain guides do exist. They are people who know the mountain. I have known of gifted individuals who are best approached by a given person who knows the difficult route through and can be relied on to bring about the desired result.

Unusual people demand unusual approaches. The question is: does the organization possess the flexibility to cope with special situations and special people?

The options here are limited. One is to engage people in a type of employment contract that is outside the system; not a 'job', as such, but a bilateral contract with a central objective at its core. Some creative individuals are keener on employment security than is commonly realized. They need the security but not the rigidity that usually goes with it. There is therefore a case for considering negotiable and renewable bilateral contracts. For those who are less interested in employment security than in securing a just reward for their 'intellectual property rights', time can be transformed into share capital or a royalty. By such a formula a useful role can be found for the brilliant maverick.

Another option is to establish a career path that is acceptable for a gifted person within the organization. Gifted people need challenges: when these are no longer in view they look for jobs elsewhere. That is why much greater use can be made of internal transfer to retain employee interest and to extract more of value for use in all the various parts of the enterprise. In this context information technology helps in advertising the contribution possibilities of the individual as well as identifying suitable openings for someone with a particular talent.

A third option is to establish a non-managerial position which carries a recognizable title and status level along with a suitable salary. In many organizations advancement is possible only by carrying increased managerial responsibility. Yet some non-managerial appointments can make a major contribution to the fortunes of the enterprise. An example of such a title in one multinational is Research Associate, a position seen as the equivalent of a Fellow of a College. Titles are important because they signify recognition and appreciation and in turn bring about loyalty. Clearly there is room for other titles, which can help to retain the interest of the very talented person, and which demand further exploration.

Developing potential

Not all talented people are difficult to manage. There is another type of talent, whose contrasting merit lies in a broad outlook and personal versatility. Such a person will succeed in a range of situations and roles – just as in a sports team, where there is on the one hand a talented star and on the other hand a player whose strength lies in setting things up for other players. In the case of this second type of player, career development within the organization needs special attention. Those burgeoning managerial talents that are so prized in industry can only become fully recognized against a variety of backgrounds and experiences.

Planned career development, if carried out on a broad scale, involves lateral moves. Almost inevitably these create political problems in hierarchical organizations. Someone who comes in from the side disturbs the pecking order of existing relationships. People silently ask themselves: where does that person fit in? Does such an entry reduce my status, my authority, my prospects?

Such questions arise because in hierarchical organizations all relationships are cast in the framework of relative seniority. People suspect favouritism and patronage. Misgivings can be dispelled only if people see an entry merely as that of another player joining a team. The future of that player, like any other player, will depend on what that person contributes. That is something on which the players themselves will form a view.

The general point is that the dismantling of hierarchy creates conditions of fluidity in which people can move around more easily, in which talent can emerge and be recognized. The usual problem is that there is an insufficiency of talent. But occasionally there is an oversupply. What happens then? That itself becomes a problem.

Talent versus talent

Talent comes in all shapes and sizes. A person with immense drive is very different from someone with an outstanding intellect; a maverick inventor may be light years away from the possessor of business and financial acumen with qualities that make a person 'streetwise'. In general it is easier to design and run an organization that comprises average people than it is to manage a group of exceptionally talented individuals.

In some instances an organization has to be tailored to match the eccentricities of a particular star. For example, in the case of one movie star, Marilyn Monroe, her unreliability brought havoc to the making of a film and resulted in an unacceptable overrun of costs. But her consequential dismissal from the set and the cancellation of her contract with the film studios left such a gap that a new and more accommodating contract had to be drawn up. It is not, however, a precedent that most managers would care to follow.

Stars in business can be even more of a headache than in the theatrical world. They have more scope for making spontaneous decisions with far-reaching consequences that may go undetected, and uncorrected, for some time. Power and talent, put together and replicated, become an explosive force. That is why in an organization where power is well established, that risk is recognized and averted.

High talent beyond the existing power base is most appreciated when it is disempowered and poses no threat. Its existence is usually confined to a specialist function.

Occasionally, when highly talented people congregate, they hit it off with one another, especially if there is some common factor that draws them together. The more usual position is that they repel each other, which then creates a strain on the organization. Should one person be dismissed to please another? Should only one star be allowed per organization? Morally, it is an unattractive proposition. But there is something in it.

Difficulties, if foreseen, can be avoided. That is why problems are best posed before they arise. A favourite question for discussion among managers on education courses is: what is the optimum size of an organization? Answers usually take one into the numbers game, as though a head count is all that matters.

There is, however, another dimension wherein parallels can be drawn with the biological relationship between an amoeba and a nucleus. The nucleus occupies the centre-stage, as it were, of the amoeba, being surrounded by support material. Without the nucleus there would be no amoeba. So what happens when there are two nuclei? The answer is that it never happens in the same amoeba without division, a process that leads to the formation of a second amoeba.

In much the same way organizations can be regarded as the home of stars, if there are any. It may be argued that human stars are not needed – they cause more trouble than they are worth. But if a star is to be nurtured, an appropriate host organization must be created. Two stars will call for a new division. So the process of hiving off into semi-autonomous organizations will go on as new stars arise. In other words, the formation of new self-contained groups should be governed as much by the distribution of talent as by the numbers game. In each case the close associates of the star will need to be carefully selected and function well as a group. They will be working under strain, for they have a limited working life-span. When the star leaves, everything changes, for the viability of the group will be lost. For them, it will be a return to the melting pot. And the pot will have to be stirred again before another magic brew is produced.

The principle then is that organizations on occasion need to be built around exceptional players, even though this is not a principle ordinarily to be recommended.

10

The culture and the organization ─────────────

The evidence of Hermann Goering's famed remark: 'When I hear the word culture I reach for my gun' suggests that culture does not appeal to everyone. Strongly based cultures, especially those with deep roots in the arts and liberal philosophies, have always posed a threat to tyrannies and totalitarian ideologies. Culture, even in a limited sense, does not, of course, offer any comparable threat to the bureaucracies of the conventional business and public sector corporation, but it can nevertheless get in the way. An unwanted cultural pattern may give rise to unexpected behaviours that frustrate the well-laid plans of managers. At one time culture rarely occupied a place among the topics considered essential for management education. But the situation has changed. The importance of cultural differences has suddenly surfaced to occupy a leading position on the agenda of management. So what has brought about this shift of attitude?

The causal factor underlying this changing scenario, in my view, has been deregulation, as it has applied in two areas – to unrestricted movements of populations between countries; and to goods in terms of international trading, and the location of manufacturing establishments. The former type of deregulation impacts principally on public sector issues; the latter on the operations of business.

Movements of people carry with them movements of culture. Management in the public sector has always to take into account the state of public opinion, for in a democratic society the accountability of those who serve the public sector is ultimately to the public itself. The problem here is that any prevailing cultural pattern contains beneath its surface a variety of minority sub-cultures. Some of these have strident voices which, in an authoritarian hierarchy, can be suppressed or ignored. But once these voices, real or imagined, need to be heeded, it is difficult to start from common assumptions that serve as an acceptable background for action. A multicultural society loses its pre-existing traditions. If these traditions are to become the casualties of population change, new traditions will have to be built up for society to establish any form of social cohesion.

The business corporation operates in a less constrained environment. Its accountability is not to the general public but to its customers and shareholders. Workers are engaged on whatever contracts the business corporation cares to offer. It can operate any style of management within any type of organizational structure it chooses. The terms are strictly 'take it or leave it'. All is well; that is until the business corporation crosses frontiers and grows into a multinational. Only then does it run into cultural complications. It is an experience large corporations share with small businesses, of which many now trade as mini multinationals for the simple reason that, with the reduction in trade tariffs and restrictions, virtually any successful small business can suddenly find itself a player on world markets. The complications then become operational rather than political and fall into two types.

The first cultural problem concerns communication and mutual understanding, which is more than a linguistic matter. What is a clear-cut inquiry in one country can, when translated, be interpreted as an insult in another; or other meanings can be attached. English businessmen visiting the USA are coached to avoid the use of a number of everyday innocent phrases that have explicit sexual meanings in America. It is said that there is no single Japanese word for 'No'. So almost every response can be taken as indecision or a 'Yes'. In India shaking of the head, which signifies 'No' to a Westerner means 'Yes, I agree', to an Indian. The nuances and gestures have to be interpreted. Often the literal translation of words may not help. Cultural understanding is needed.

Here, I am reminded of the old English joke about the difference between an American politician and a Parisian lady: when an American politician says 'Yes', he means 'Maybe', when he says 'Maybe', he means 'No'; when a Parisian lady says 'No', she means 'Maybe', when she says 'Maybe', she means 'Yes'.

Words and conventions can often act as smokescreens hiding deeply held values and customs. Polite formalities and exchanges parry the direct conduct of business and can last so long in some quarters of the globe that frustrated businessmen return from their overseas commercial missions without any deals to report. The real meaning of this preliminary social exchange is that it serves as a means of assessing the worth of a person before any contract is entered into.

The relationship between the individual and the society needs to be fully understood in each society if the prime contact point is with individuals in foreign lands. A course of action expected from an individual can jeopardize that person's standing within the primary group, and lead to loss of face. Codes of industrial discipline are difficult to administer in an acceptable way for cultural reasons, while equally a lack of harshness can be interpreted as weakness. In some cultures a proneness to engage in cover-up, with a view to protecting either the self or colleagues, is a serious matter because suppression of information can have far-reaching operational consequences. In such cases, corporations have, to my knowledge, reversed their initial investment decisions. For example, in certain countries it has been judged too dangerous on the human front to set up chemical processing plants because the standard of close supervision by the qualified local population is too lax and the introduction of expatriates is resisted. In another case, a leading airline cancelled its plans to establish a combined service with a third-world country after doubts about a readiness to report technical faults, especially those that could be traced back to human error or negligence.

Culture: a matter of values, attitudes or behaviour?

Management has begun to have doubts on how these problems can be constructively tackled. Should the focus fall on understanding language, of correctly interpreting gestures or, more problematical still, of perceiving those attitudes and values that are part of the largely hidden culture of the work environment? And even if a broad understanding of the culture were reached, would it help? Are some cultures so firmly based that, faced with cultural incompatibility with the parent body, they successfully resist all outside pressures?

Such questions raise some important theoretical issues. But management, always pragmatic in its approach, needs a firm starting point from which it can move forward. Happily, one already exists. One industrial, and unashamedly behavioural, definition of culture is: 'the way we do things round here'. So the problem soon reduces to recognizing the gap between 'the way we do things at Head Office' and 'the way they do things at other places'.

The presumption in the past has been 'to get them to do the things over there the way we do things here'. This, which I will call Method One, aimed at replicating the methods and policies of the Centre by appointing trusty lieutenants to command the outposts of Empire. When that didn't work, for what was now seen as cultural problems with the natives, Method Two came into operation. Method Two set out to change values. It was not done obtrusively. Instead, values were solemnly presented as a collective expression of the firm, almost as though it carried the mandate of having been voted upon. In reality, there was nothing open for discussion. It amounted to no more than a style of behaviour favoured by the Chief Executive, even if the establishment would proclaim it an example of positive leadership.

When both methods failed to meet their goals, it was time for a rethink. The only option left was to adopt Method Three: to accept that 'they do things differently over there' and to adjust strategic policies to the operational demands of different cultural settings. There are four distinctive, though not necessarily mutually exclusive, types of culture that are very resistant to foreign influence.

One is the authoritarian culture, where things get done only by finding the person with status to make decisions. Should that person be absent from the scene, no one else is prepared to take over responsibility. The leaderless group does not believe that it is sanctioned to act on its own behalf. Inertia is not a function of laziness but of lack of self-confidence. Given that cultural position, the operational effectiveness of policies fashioned at the Centre depends on finding key individuals holding the reins of power.

A second culture is the kinship culture. Paid positions are distributed as a matter of priority to members of the family. Merit and suitability are secondary matters. Organizations that interfere with this set of priorities will in practice be ignored.

A third pattern, very prevalent in some parts of the world, is the consensus culture. No one individual is empowered to make decisions or, even if empowered, would care to make important decisions without further consultation. The referral process becomes protracted. But when eventually an agreed decision emerges, it becomes totally binding.

A fourth pattern is the bribe culture. No one can be expected to do anything without a sweetener. Regulations and bureaucracy create functional impediments: they are designed to obstruct but can always be overcome, and indeed can only be overcome, with money passed to the obstructionist.

It would be absurd to treat an authoritarian and kinship culture as if it were a consensus culture, or to treat a consensus culture as though it were a bribe culture. Multinationals have often done better by leaving such tricky operational questions to a Mr Fix-it. Mr Fix-it knows the ropes. Given the ends, Mr Fix-it knows enough about the culture to know which means to employ.

From multinationals to transnationals

It has to be conceded that many multinationals are not very happy about employing a Mr Fix-it or assigning money to a slush fund. Multinationals have their own cultural values. In the case of reputable corporations, supporting corruption is seen as an indictment of their own ethics.

When the culture of a Head Office Corporation comes up against the divergent ways of business in a particular country, something has to give way. If the conflict continues, there are losers and no winners and the investor is certainly the loser. The basic mistake is that strategic and operational policies are treated as transferable as a single package that can be introduced in every land in a more or less standard way. In the case of businesses with few parameters, as in the fast food restaurant chains with a limited product range, straight transference of the standard package may work out. All that may be required is close attention to a few crucial details. It becomes a different matter when the same approach is applied to complex businesses, where transfer means making assumptions that cannot be checked physically.

Even well-intended compromise approaches have a disappointing track record. In my own home city a multinational in science-based business, and with a strong presence in Japan, believed that a cross-fertilization of ideas and practices would bring about the best of both worlds for the Group. Accordingly it sent a few of its most talented young people to Japan and imported some of theirs to England. What happened was not what had been expected. After a period the English scientists in Japan started behaving just like the Japanese and the Japanese, for their part, adopted typical English practices: the culture had simply absorbed the transplants. The story is reminiscent of colonial days when a common complaint against isolated expatriates abroad was that they had 'gone native'.

There is only one remaining option for a complex business in a foreign field: it is to give up the idea of replication; to give up the idea of close control, of domination, of changing the culture in the desired direction. Gradually, multinationals have stumbled towards the winning formula. It was to send over only a few liaison expatriates, while selecting with care and ultimately relying on locals to manage. In that way cultural transformation was unnecessary; or, if it came about to some moderate degree, it was an unforced process. But the approach had to be more than a gesture. The locals had to have decision-making power in their own right. They were colleagues, not junior members of a hierarchy.

It is this new formula that has given rise to the transnational. Multinationals have started transforming themselves into trans-nationals. Whereas multinationals were centred on Head Offices, transnationals have become multicentred. Whereas multinationals imposed their chosen progeny on peripheral establishments, trans-nationals have set out to utilize the best talents from all the geographical spheres in which they operate. This transformation has not been easy, for it has depended on modifying the nature of the organization at the heart of the enterprise.

The culture, the organization and behaviour

Historically, it cannot be true that local cultures always win over intruders, for the reverse can certainly hold. That is how empires have been built up, whose cultures still retain their traits and vitality long after their original regimes have vanished. What now has to be considered is whether values created the organization or the organization created the values.

It is customary to hold that values come first. A nation professes its adherence to Christianity or Islam or democracy or Communism or capitalism, or to some other generic system of beliefs, and from there spring its practices. This is not however a theory that historical analysis bears out.

If people are to be judged by how they behave rather than by how they describe themselves and their values, it is revealing just how far the discrepancies can stretch. The Christian precept to 'love thy neighbour' and to 'turn the other cheek' did not hold back the bloodbath of the Crusades, with its acts of genocide committed against the main Islamic enemy along with smaller, Jewish and Christian, communities encountered on the road to the Holy Land; nor did the Christian precepts prove any impediment to the tortures of the Inquisition. Nearer to our present times, the gulags of the Soviet Union became the destination of anyone falling foul of the Communist dictatorship; yet Communism's main thrust came from opposition to Tsarist absolutism and the ideology that fuelled the revolution was value driven.

The values in these two instances failed to retain their grip on behaviour. So the question arises: what force overrides these values? The answer, I would claim, is 'Organization'.

A key to understanding the human setback of the Middle Ages lies in appreciating that the declining power of the Roman Empire was saved from total moral collapse by its alliance with the up-and-coming Christian Church. That alliance produced the Holy Roman Empire. The character of Christianity now underwent an organizational transformation. From being a communistic and pacifist gathering in which women had played an increasingly important part, the Church took on the form of a military-type hierarchy of which the Head was 'infallible'. Women became downgraded in terms of their allowed roles, even being debarred from displaying their musical vocal gifts as soloists in church, their place being taken by castrati.

The way in which Christianity has been practised throughout its history has depended on the organization that lay behind it. The values have remained relatively unchanged, because the Bible has remained the fount of its authority. Nevertheless, that source has been unable to prevent values from being overridden by the behaviour demanded by the organization.

Communism, too, followed much the same path, although it failed ultimately to reform itself. The original slogan of the Russian revolution was 'all power to the soviets', the soviets being village assemblies. The cry asserted the right of local people to uphold their democratic rights and to resist the absolutist nature of tsarist rule. The principle of 'democratic centralism' implied a new advance in Organization. In reality the phrase proved cover for a new highly centralized tyranny under which a Solo Leader ruled supreme. Countless numbers of dissidents and innocent people were subsequently to perish in gulags before the whole moribund organizational system collapsed, virtually of its own accord.

The character of an organization can destroy the ideals which created a following in the first place. However, a well designed organization can foster new working values that have a positive effect on behaviour. In the sphere of political organization democracy provides an example. It is said that no democracy has ever declared war on another democracy. In contrast, where dictators are in command, military conflicts can certainly be expected.

In summary, cultures can be changed, not in the first place by training or education nor by the exercise of force, but by bringing about an organizational transformation. The appropriate organization will in time create a culture of its own. It will be a culture where behaviour develops predictable patterns, which does not mean that the employees all share the same personal values. In a cosmopolitan society personal values will vary immensely. But how those values are expressed in terms of behaviour will depend on the pressures ultimately exerted by the shape of the organization.

11

Strategic leadership comes of age ——————

The distinction between strategic and operational management may seem artificial to many managers. In the case of small businesses, in particular, their very strength would seem to lie in the ability to treat and manage the business as a whole. In practice the same manager handles both strategic and operational functions. Not that managers of small businesses possess the resources to act otherwise, even if that was an accepted goal. Managers of large business empires, for their part, do have the necessary resources to bring about the separation of functions, but are nevertheless inclined to take the same view as managers of small businesses. Even in the larger setting they like to view and manage the totality of what goes on and position themselves to have a finger in every pie. The crucial difference between the two situations, however, is that while managers of small businesses do succeed in that way, managers of large empires generally do not. For reasons explained in Chapter 5 they run, almost inevitably, into the phenomenon of the single channel capacity bottleneck. They are short of the attention-time available to deal with matters that require protracted consideration. In the event, strategic decisions tend to be made impulsively and treated as an extension of operational behaviour.

Leaving aside practical circumstances, the case for separating strategic management from operational management in the larger organization could be made on personal grounds alone. There are certain issues that need very clever people capable of dealing with complexity, possessing vision and the motivation to work towards a distant objective. They should be prepared to take all the painstaking steps that progress demands and to explore a variety of routes that involve journeys up cul-de-sacs before finally discovering the best path. In contrast, there is an entirely different range of matters (in truth the bulk of those that appear on the agenda of management) that demand quick judgement and equally quick action plus effective communication with those contributing at the various interfaces that precede the decision process.

Executives who are ideal for one of these scenarios are, almost by definition, less suited for the other scenario. Hence there is a natural division of functions that correspond with the natural temperamental differences between executives.

Managing in an age of discontinuity

Even if there were no other reason for developing a focus on strategic management, as a special form of management, the uncertainties of living in an age of deregulated markets and growing international competition are bound to thrust the subject to the fore. Most corporations, whether private or public, have to face the painful reality that any stability achieved in the present has no guarantee of lasting. It means that the corporation has to perform, as it were, a juggling act, keeping three balls in the air all at the same time. Those three balls correspond to managing the present, managing the near future and managing the only partly foreseeable future.

The further one reaches into the future, the more uncertain become the facts and the range of issues that have to be considered. The essence of the partly foreseeable is that clear-cut facts and issues are inextricably linked with intangibles that also have to be brought into the equation. The way in which these are best combined poses a conundrum. The fact that there are unforeseeable elements in the situation is what accounts for the protracted nature of strategic deliberations. Were decision-making time to be reduced, it is almost certain that the focus would fall on the known, the certain and the incontrovertible at the expense of the seemingly nebulous. Almost certainly that would be no advantage. Hastening the decision-making process leads to unbalanced decisions.

That is something I learned when working on Total Quality Control. The general position was that what was measurable would be immediately measured, thereby creating a sense of corporate security, while the difficult to measure, such as the physical properties of materials or their ageing characteristics would receive scant scrutiny and sometimes no scrutiny at all. The assumptions that the measurable is more important than the unmeasurable, the tangible more important than the intangible, and the clearly foreseeable more important than what can be foreseen as a possibility, die hard.

The complex environment that forms the background for the making of strategic decisions demands an unhurried approach. Once that approach is put into effect, various unwanted consequences are prone to follow in their wake. Urgencies become deferred. The corporation becomes a giant with its head in a whirl and its feet in clay. Its brain is no longer large enough to cope with all its limbs. If truth be told, it needs more brains rather than a larger single brain. And more brains mean more people thinking rather than one person thinking more.

The limits of intervention

The general slowing up involved by the intrinsic nature of strategic thinking has important implications for managerial organization. If problems are to be overcome, strategic managers must be freed from matters that press for immediate attention. They can no longer expect to manage everything that is going on without incurring the accusation of being either slipshod on strategic thinking, or slow-moving on matters calling for rapid action. Faced with the dilemma of veering one way or the other, managers face a no-win situation.

The only feasible remedy is to reconstruct the organization in a way that ensures that executives are freed from any intrinsic conflict on the use to which their time is put. This calls for two steps to be taken. The first involves a new division of managerial labour. Executives who work on major issues and problem areas imbued with high levels of uncertainty should not be expected to deal with the everyday issues that typically confront busy line managers. The second is that major issues should not have a stop-watch suspended over them, for matters that can affect the future and very survival of the corporation need depth of consideration.

I have postulated, where the size of the corporation permits, a formal separation between strategic and operational management, believing that quite different skills are involved in these areas. These two levels of contribution are not, however, synonymous with senior and middle management. A senior, experienced and effective operational manager can be expected to make a bigger contribution than a younger and less experienced strategic executive and may be expected to earn more. The important difference between these two modes of management lies in their focus. In the case of operational management the issues force themselves to the fore, sometimes giving rise to what is known as crisis management; in the case of strategic management the issues have to be unearthed, a process that makes demands on a proactive intellect.

The importance of strategic management is easily underrated. Many an issue that has not pressed for attention proves in the event to be vital. For example, I have known businesses that export much of their output prosper or decline due to 'chance' shifts in the exchange rates of currencies, for which the business was unprepared. 'Chance' political factors can, again, have dramatic effects on a business. These events that can take a company by surprise are often treated as unforeseeable by those who believe that business and politics don't mix: more correctly they were unforeseen. So, too, industrial disputes that have crippled a corporation have often taken management by surprise. Perhaps the most general of the uncertainties in the conduct of business is the continuous change in the state of the market which can swing from shortages to glut and back to shortages again; or the swings of fashion which can dictate the direction of demand for consumer goods. The most feared change is a steady trend in downward demand. Reaction to a saturation of markets cannot be made suddenly except by ceasing to trade. Positive reaction calls for forward thinking on products or services that can take the place of those that are being displaced. Lead times are inevitably long, which is why strategic anticipation has become such an important skill in the current era.

All these and other areas that pose uncertainty about the future overlap with one another. Hence the teams of executives who tackle these various issues need to overlap too in their working sessions. To believe that strategic managers can be subsumed under a single linear chain of command is to court absurdity, for then the process in arriving at decisions is even slower. Strategic teams need team empowerment more than any other group if it means that potential crises are to be averted in time.

Organizing the strategic group

The crucial issue is how the strategic function should be organized. The old army distinction between line and staff officers is here a sound one. The staff officers are the strategic managers, a title that might be preferred since it more aptly describes their function. But it is a mistake to believe that a strategic team should be confined to people with strategic skills, just as we have also learned that creative people on their own do not form a creative team.

What actually happens when you put strategic people together was well conveyed to us by our experience with business games on Strategic Leadership Courses in the UK and, more especially, in Australia. The executives with the most strategic outlook were those whose style and orientation put them into those team-role categories which we termed Monitor Evaluators and Plants. As part of the design for learning, we put those who were most conspicuous in these team roles all together in the same team and observed their progress. They analysed, they argued, they debated; and their results fell short of what might have been reasonably expected for clever people. The trouble was that while they were closeted in their syndicate rooms, they tended to lose touch with what was going on outside.

A well balanced strategic team contains not only strategic thinkers but a reasonable mix of other people. Professional specialists and operational personnel also have something of value to contribute to such a team. A few companies have reported benefits from mixing directors with blue-collar workers on projects where the interface between strategy and mode of operation is crucial. And why not? In a hierarchical organization it would constitute an affront to protocol. But a delayered organization is characterized by free-floating and inter-acting cells rather than by separated levels and therein lies its strength.

The rule for a strategic team is that it should be assembled by a strategic convenor whose personal presence ensures that its decisions are binding on management as a whole. As the team is empowered, its composition needs to reflect an appropriate balance for arriving at decisions that could have far-reaching consequences. Given several strategic managers, there can be a number of teams sitting con-currently and conducting simultaneous but not similar business. The range of matters that such an organization can encompass is thereby greatly extended over the limiting confines of the single-line authority of a hierarchy.

Filling gaps in the strategic team

One criticism commonly levelled at corporations is that they have become in-bred. Policies of recruitment that set out to match the image and culture of the corporation result in cloning. If mistakes are made, everyone goes along with them, for no one wishes to be seen as out-of-line. Cloning usually stems from operational needs. Typical tasks and typical activities result in the selection of people best fitted to carry them out. To outsiders, their uniformity affords an appearance of being 'typical company people'.

If new strategies are to be developed and the corporation is not to stagnate, typical company people will not be the ones to make it happen. If there were any lateral thinkers in the corporation, they will already have left. There will therefore be a dearth of appropriate personnel. So how is the gap to be filled?

One means is already favoured. It is to appoint non-executive directors. Many of these are retirees from other companies who have made themselves available for post-retirement, part-time appoint-ments. Certainly that is one way of filling the breach. But other ways need to be explored. Not all new members introduced into the strategic team should be specified as elder statesmen. So what other possibilities exist?

Before a corporation looks to outsiders, it needs to ensure that it has not overlooked insiders. Information technology now allows one to examine a database on the team-role profile of all employees and their tendency to make specific types of contribution at work. Technically it is a short step to find someone with a fitting aptitude who can be invited to join a strategic team. Such assignment can be temporary; it can be treated as an exercise in career development and need not denote a claim to seniority. It is only by exploring the untested talents of promising individuals that a corporation can properly evaluate its human resources. This line of approach is seldom employed, because temporary and lateral movements of personnel within the system are inhibited by notions of seniority and bypass considerations of specific ability. Putting an unexpected person into an unexpected position creates controversy. Hence people stay locked in their narrow cells, called 'jobs'. That is why a new sort of organization needs to be set up and understood before people's career aspirations can be turned into some form of progressive reality.

The third means of importing talent into a strategic team is to create a place for consultants. There are now many people who prefer to be self-employed, and for whom a corporation would have difficulty anyway in finding a full-time appointment. There is more security for the self-employed in taking on several varied assignments than in becoming over-dependent on a big contract from a single client. The economic advantages in such an arrangement serve both parties, the part-time consultant and the corporation that needs new blood.

The nature of the strategic function

The importance of strategic issues is that they take account of a wider number of variables than normally enter into a discussion on a particular matter. That process means they have the potential to override seemingly rational decisions based on limited information. Strategic decisions and operational decisions may not conflict, but, if they do, the former take precedence.

Matters of strategy and leadership belong together. There is certainly much current interest in strategic leadership. In some quarters this is taken to imply a need for a clever Mr Big. People readily believe, and it may often be true, that difficult problems are best farmed out to those with brains. However, the problems raised by strategic issues at the managerial level are fraught with conceptual and situational complexity. Their multidimensional nature embodies a social dimension, which means they stand a better chance of being solved when handled by a team, especially if the implementation of decisions necessitates commitment from others.

It is doubtful whether corporations, public or private, are well served in the long run by relying on one strategic leader. Yet they certainly need a strategic function capable of providing leadership; one that can make firm, and sometimes unpopular, decisions. Of necessity, high-order strategic talents must reside somewhere within the team without being allowed to unbalance the team's capacity for wide managerial responsibility. The presence of someone in a staff or strategic role will be sufficient to make its decisions 'official'. But the ratification of any decision should depend not just on the personal standpoint of its most talented strategic member but on endorsement by the team itself.

12

The organization of public affairs _____

Whenever I bring my gaze to bear on the field of public affairs, I find signs of crisis everywhere. The catalogue of unresolved and recurring social and political problems suggests that humans are not very good at dealing with large-scale organizational issues. *Homo sapiens* operated throughout the greater part of the span of its life on earth in bands of hunters and gatherers seldom exceeding one hundred members. Groups of this size and less still today exhibit vitality and cooperation. But once groups have grown to the point that most members are unknown to each other, human organizations become troubled.

The largest human organizations are associated with government. One general symptom of the problem of achieving stability is the steadily increasing proportion of the Gross Domestic Product swallowed up by government expenditure. This rise cannot go on forever without generating some form of ultimate breakdown in the economic and social order. Signs of a taxpayers' revolt are much in evidence. Whenever a referendum is held that focuses specifically on tax or when tax-cutting figures strongly in an election campaign, the electors will opt for tax-cutting: there are clearly limits to the amount of income that income earners are prepared to sacrifice in order that it may be spent by government. Yet an equally strong tide is pulling in the opposite direction, for the public looks to government for solutions on all matters of public concern. The list is formidable. It includes inflation, crime, unemployment, pollution, the depletion of resources (including forests), global warming and the standard of public services. The electorate expects government to come up with solutions. The struggle between those who want less government and those who expect more from government is never-ending.

Yet there is one field from which government can never escape responsibility, for it constitutes the most potentially threatening of the dangers that can arise from any failure to manage public affairs effectively: it is the containment of conflicts between ethnic, linguistic, religious and ideological minorities. Such conflicts, which can spill over national borders, present a continuing threat to the peace of the world, for as problems are solved in one place they break out in another.

Human beings seem to possess well developed abilities for social organization when in small and medium-sized groups. Yet in larger groups it is another matter. That is where ants and bees possess sophisticated systems that surpass those of humans and other mammals, as Chapter 4 has shown. When it comes to regulating our public affairs, we humans can at least plead that we are no worse than other mammals. In reality we are broadly comparable. Mammals build up their own system of organization and control through dominance. The alpha male dominates the animal pack, often achieving sole breeding rights. Dominance between packs also figures in the defence and extension of territories. In the same way dictators, after establishing their territories, acquire empires.

The limited advance in organization achieved by humans is that the alpha male has found a way of exercising dominance over groups larger that the immediate pack. The method is to create a hierarchy of relative dominance. So in the past large chunks of the world have been ruled by tyrants and smaller chunks by lesser tyrants. And smaller tyrants have bigger tyrants on their backs to bite them.

In recent times there has been a general revolt against tyrannical autocracies. The outcome has been an advance towards a more advanced form of political organization called democracy. Democracy has opened up the process of international consultation in step with the way in which it has fostered political consultations within a country. Fair progress has been made towards the civilized regulation of international affairs and international conduct. All that falls on the credit balance.

However, a great deal of leadership is built on the old model. An elected autocracy has replaced a tyrannical autocracy. The frontiers and provinces of the State along with the bureaucracies that run it have scarcely changed. Centralized power in populous States has become more strongly entrenched through the substantial tax revenues it raises. Such revenues are then turned into expenditure with all its consequential hold over the recipients of that expenditure. The power so generated, along with an all-pervading associated set of standard systems and regulations, enables Mr Big to be bigger than ever. Yet Mr Big often owes his democratic mandate not to the majority, which his mandate would imply, but to being the representative of the largest minority. A quasi-autocratic democracy is built on an electoral system under which the winner takes all. The losing minorities, often comprising distinct ethnic, linguistic or religious groups, are thereby permanently disenfranchised from the exercise of power and control over their own environment. For them democracy is an illusion.

Local government too is fast becoming an illusion in terms of its capacity to act effectively in fulfilling its role in addressing local problems. The laws, regulations and procedures are broadly determined by central government. Local government is there mainly to administer what is laid down, a point that is certainly recognized by electors. At the time of local elections, swings in voting behaviour have everything to do with the way in which central government is perceived and little to do with how well local government is performing.

Correcting the organizational flaw: towards devolution

The problem facing mankind is whether it can now go forward to reach a system of social and political organization as advanced and as stable as that of bees and ants with their highly devolved systems. Our genetic inheritance suggests we are more poorly equipped for this task than our diminutive cohabitees on this planet. But at least we can learn. That is what humans are good at doing. The initial need is to understand where the mechanisms are failing in the management of public affairs.

The first observation is that government possesses all the faults associated with the large multi-tiered business corporation headed by Mr Big and his associates. If there are differences they are fairly superficial. In one case heads may roll at a general election and in the other at a shareholders' meeting. When a new boss takes over, the organization remains much the same.

If the similarities are more striking than the differences, there is at least one difference that has important consequences for Organization. It stems from the fact that government is far more intent on standardization. Business is not overly concerned with how its subsidiaries operate provided they make a profit. Government, however, formulates and operates programmes designed to be part of a national system. No variations are permitted to take account of local circumstances save in exceptional cases. Governmental bureaucracy means rules and regulations are more important than discretion or judgement. It is a strange paradox that *Homo sapiens*, the most intelligent of all living creatures, should choose a formula which deliberately excludes the use of intelligence in the management of public affairs.

How decisions are made

Given that governmental programmes are standardized to the point of rigidity, the crucial matter now becomes how they are initiated. The vast powers of government are exercised from relatively simple starting points.

The first follows the alpha male route. The strongest member of the government pack dominates discussion and seeks to put a personal stamp on a new policy. It is then passed on to civil servants to be enacted along the lines the minister has chosen. When a new minister comes in, which is fairly often, the policy is revised in some minor detail but in a way that is sufficient to allow the new minister to leave his own personal dominant mark.

The second option, which ostensibly seems more democratic, has its origins in the atmosphere at the party conference. The good party orator is one who can arouse emotions by jeering at enemies, lampooning opponents and can offer immediately comforting solutions to the problems that concern people. If the solutions that are adumbrated appeal and raise cheers, a new figure appears on the political scene, who may eventually become a Mr Big. But this is almost secondary to the fact that a new policy is launched. The gauge for determining which policy wins most support is the so-called clapometer. This refers to an instrument developed by the media for measuring the level of applause.

Unfortunately the emotions of crowd behaviour are notoriously poor pointers to good decision-making. The solutions that appeal to party conferences are regularly contradicted by the results of research. Criminologists do not concur with the view that capital punishment and harsher penalties reduce crime, nor do economists find that job protection measures reduce unemployment nor that trade protection measures serve the interests of industry in the long run. A policy of informed resource allocation based on devolving decision-making to responsible people on how limited resources are best used is a more effective way of controlling public expenditure. Unfortunately proposals that have their origin in a combination of expert opinion and research generally lack the sort of immediate appeal that is likely to arouse cheers at a party conference.

If the control and direction of public affairs are to continue to depend on either Mr Big or the party clapometer, the prospects for human society are bleak.

Fortunately there are other ways in which public affairs can be strategically handled. But this means getting back to the basics of good organization.

The interface between the strategic and the operational

Most governmental measures are devised without any close consultation with the people who are going to run the programme. That is because in a multilevel hierarchy the senior and the operating levels are too far apart ever to meet. That is the typical fault of the large organization.

The problem can be illustrated with reference to fishing. Fish stocks are becoming exhausted in many parts of the world. Methods of conserving fish stocks are considered by international organizations and by government and plans are drawn up accordingly. The methods of control introduced revolve round a quota on the catch that can be landed and on the individual size of the fish that can be sold. That would appear to offer comprehensive protection to younger, less developed fish. But almost immediately fishermen find the simplest way of meeting the regulations. The same quantity of fish are caught as before. The only difference is that the best are kept for sale while the rest are thrown back dead into the sea.

Another method of control is to restrict the number of days in which fishing boats can put to sea. However, in the case of trawlers, research indicates that it is not the number of days at sea that is critical so much as observation of a close season on particular breeding grounds.

The people who know most about fishing are fishermen, along with a handful of ichthyologists. If government were delayered and downsized, it would be reasonable to expect those round the decision-making table to include one or two figures wearing deep blue woolly pullovers. Fishermen and senior civil servants use different styles of verbal communication. Exchanging information and views can there-fore present a social no less than an organizational challenge.

The conspicuous disjunction between the policy-makers and the implementers of policies was brought home to me during a period when my colleagues and I were developing experimental manpower programmes under the auspices of the Industrial Training Research Unit. The government had set up training programmes in urban areas of high unemployment to enable those without work to secure other jobs and had also set up an inspection directorate to ensure that training standards were met. However, those who completed their training found themselves in competition in the labour market with workers who already possessed work experience in relevant skills. These latter workers were preferred by employers for the vacancies on offer. The government then carried out a cost/benefit analysis, the results of which showed that the programmes in areas of high unemployment were the 'least efficient'. The programme we were observing was then closed down. But with a different approach it could have been saved.

One of the more enterprising trainers showed the way forward. Where others were failing, he had succeeded in securing jobs for his trainees by establishing contacts with employers, examining the nature of the work they undertook, finding jobs on which the trainees could gain some temporary work experience and then building on the opportunity when the employer found a good fit between the trainee presented and the demands of the work that was normally under-taken. However, this improved strategy had to be discontinued as the Government Inspectorate discovered that the trainer was neglecting his official training duties in favour of these other non-prescribed activities. Hence the trainer was stopped from doing what was more effective.

In the health field, another débâcle arose from the attempts of the government to discover the costs of various medical operations with a view to discovering the most efficient, i.e. low cost, units. Startling differences appeared. But the differences were mainly explicable in terms of the lack of application on the part of some of the nurses who were given the task of completing the various forms to be fed into the computer.

One well-known failure in the general approach to an important problem, now encountered in most developed countries, relates to the payment of unemployment benefit. That is set at a standard level by government. But the level can never be right. For some, the level represents a means of escape from the rigours of work and any shortfall in income is made up by unofficial working. I once gave a lift to a graduate hitch-hiker who had given up his job as a computer programmer in London in favour of unemployment pay in his home town. There he was able to combine leisure with remunerative activities in the evenings with a pop group. To counter abuse, a low level of unemployment benefit increases the pressure to find a job. But that produces another type of problem. The genuine job-seeker, living in an area of high living costs, can be reduced to distress and poverty, especially if financial commitments have been entered into before the loss of a job.

All these examples of failed policies should not be attributed to some error of judgement at the top, nor to the inefficiency of some local bureaucrat. There is a deeper explanation. The flaws are due to an organization that is intrinsically unworkable. Nor is it likely that the existing system could ever become workable whatever improvements were made.

Regenerating public organizations: the three Ds

The faults of government in terms of the organizational principles developed in this book are easy, in an intellectual sense, to identify and correct. They are no different from those that beset large corporations. However, there are a number of special considerations to be borne in mind.

Government, like corporations, works better when the three Ds are applied: delayering, downsizing and devolution. However, the three Ds give rise to a fourth – dynamite. Devolution entails local people making local decisions. That is the force that necessarily blows up standardization. There could under this system be no standard unemployment rates of benefit nor would claims on eligibility be the same. Such a revolution would have predictable consequences. Claimants would relocate to areas offering the most attractive benefits. That is what happened in New York when those from the deep South and from Puerto Rico discovered the new Eldorado beckoning for those without prospects. The result was that New York moved into bankruptcy.

If local areas are to be freed from central control and are to use assets to best advantage, they need the powers to decide who is and who is not eligible to receive the benefits that go with residency and citizenship. That moves the political scene very much nearer to that prevailing in Switzerland.

When devolution involves handling substantial sums of public money and allows a measure of discretion on the merits and demerits of recipients, the door is left ajar for corruption to creep in. In this respect standardized government programmes hold an advantage: with little room for discretion, there is little room for corruption.

The problem that has to be faced is how a system can be developed that provides for local decision-making, so allowing latitude of interpretation in individual cases, while safeguarding civic integrity and responsibility. Can these two goals be reconciled?

Election or selection?

What would seem crucial in this context is the method of election or selection. In the normal course of events the adversarial nature of party elections places the emphasis on the party label and distracts attention from the personal qualities of the candidate. That is how so many unworthy candidates achieve political office. But proper selection means assessing fitness for office. When selection has primacy of importance over election, the political affiliations of the candidate are more in the nature of a backdrop. What matters is the candidate's personal worth.

If there is to be confidence in the capacity of representatives of the people to make important decisions in the public interest, there is room for a new slogan: there can be no election without selection and no selection without election. The Athenians may have believed that the gods were the best selectors. That may be true in the sense that normal people do not select too well.

My belief that a better system exists for ensuring the entry into office of suitable people who are also properly representative of a cross-section of society is founded on personal experience in the appointment of lay magistrates. The method differs from those normally used in bringing about public representation. My introduction to the subject followed a strange course.

One day I received a telephone call from someone who asked if I would be willing to carry out some public duties that would make a limited demand on my time. The nature of those duties could not be mentioned on the telephone but would be discussed when we met. In due course I learned that I had been nominated to become the first lay member on the Lord Chancellor's Advisory Committee for the City of Cambridge and for the County of Cambridgeshire. In the early days the whole matter was surrounded in secrecy. No-one was to know of my position, since it was presumed that any member of the Committee could become a target for coercion. Later the policy changed and the appointment became public knowledge.

With the exception of myself the Committee consisted of a small group of experienced magistrates. The aim was to recommend to the Lord Chancellor candidates for appointment to the Magistracy after taking account of the Lord Chancellor's guidelines. Suitable candidates needed to possess an appropriate set of personal qualities but also needed to meet certain quota requirements. These covered political voting behaviour, occupation, age and sex. The application form was designed to elicit the necessary background information including usual voting behaviour. That question in any other circumstance would have been regarded as an unwarranted intrusion into personal matters. All candidates needed to be nominated by public bodies, and to be supported by proposers and seconders, although later self-nomination was allowed. Shortlisted candidates were then given a searching interview by three members of the Committee. If their personal qualities were judged to be suitable, they were then given a second interview by three other members of the Committee. The second interview differed from the first in that case studies were presented on which the candidate was invited to comment. Here the approach was being assessed rather than the merits of specific judgements, for appointee magistrates were subsequently given judicial training.

There were two things pertinent to the management of public affairs that I learned from a decade of experience in this work. The first related to the high personal qualities and integrity of the candidates who succeeded in passing through all the selection stages and into the Magistracy. These were people who were performing a valuable public service without any form of remuneration other than their expenses. The second related to the capacity of members of the Committee to arrive at judgements without fear or favour. Due to the obligatory need to state 'normal voting behaviour' it was possible to know the political affiliations of each member of the Committee. Yet when a candidate of the same political persuasion appeared before the Committee, there was never a temptation to depart from impartiality. There were occasions when some notable member of the local Establishment was turned down for the Magistracy. But, in response to the challenge presented in these cases, members of the Committee never wavered in their professional judgement.

The lesson is that it is possible to find able and upright members of the community who are prepared to act in the public interest. That possibility is, however, contingent on a satisfactory process being found for combining election with selection. These processes are better handled through several stages rather than at a single stage, where gross mistakes can easily be made.

Opportunities linked with local decisions and local enterprise

For the devolution of government to be properly carried out, the command and control relationship between central government to local government would have to be dismantled. This would entail abandoning standardization of many social security entitlements. Local government is better placed to decide how the total financial cake should be divided, where local priorities lie and to distinguish between worthy recipients and fraudulent claimants. I have little doubt that worthy citizens can be found to make these judgements given a better system for judging fitness for public office.

A change in any one sub-system impacts on another. The public domain is full of sub-systems. Change therefore has to be approached with some perspective on how it affects the total pattern. Abandoning standardization in the treatment of beneficiaries would mean that bounty-seekers would gravitate to the more indulgent areas. That in turn would heighten consciousness of who were the insiders and who the intruders. A vista begins to open up of belongingness, of a return to the clan or, as has been noted earlier, to the canton. By this means community is resurrected. And it is through the renewal of community that social morality is revitalized.

The breakdown and scattering of the extended family, however, means that community can never be the sole organizational reference point for the management of social security. Federal government programmes will have to exist alongside local programmes. But the former will need to be specifically contracted into. Individuals will therefore have a choice. They will need to decide as to which of the two systems they will belong.

A complaint that can arise when local government possesses the powers to formulate its own decisions on how local problems should be tackled concerns anomalies. People will be treated in different ways in different places because local authorities will reach different decisions on how similar problems should be addressed. The facilities belonging to institutions of a certain character in one place will be lacking in another. Local people will complain but they will also point with pride at what they believe is done better in their locality than elsewhere.

In an earlier book – *The Job Promoters: A Journey To a New Profession* – I have developed a number of strategies and methods that I believe would yield better returns on public expenditure than the routine payment of unemployment benefit to the jobless. I have also described institutions that handled difficult problems with consummate skill and success. However, so long as central government controls the purse strings and operates its totalitarian programmes, the lessons of local progress can never be learned. If a local programme proves cost-effective in getting the jobless back into jobs or in creating new employment opportunities by providing good nursery facilities for the development of small new enterprises, the overwhelming financial gain accrues to central government. The costs are incurred locally and the benefits centrally. This cybernetic fault lies at the heart of organizational failure.

Revving the evolutionary engine

The peak periods and localities in the history of civilization in terms of architecture, art, music, science and literature underline the enormous contribution of the city States and independent kingdoms – Miletus, Athens, Corinth, Venice, Genoa, Bologna, Florence, Siena, Assisi, Bruges, the cities of the Hanseatic League and so on. These civic entities were able to operate on a human scale where initiatives and enterprise brought their own rewards and were not easily stifled. Their problem was that they excited the envy and ambitions of larger neighbours. When it comes to military confrontation bigness pays. Larger States swallow smaller ones. The world is now composed of strong powers that exercise military might, euphemistically termed Defence. The only defence that is truly required, especially by smaller States, is collective security. Yet the United Nations finds it difficult to fund collective security operations or to establish a permanent force with terms of reference that enables it to act quickly. Sophisticated military forces kept by States not threatened by neighbours absorb huge sums of public money.

The bigness of central government, official bureaucracy, the standardization of public systems, high taxation and heavy public expenditure are all interconnected. The devolution of political power would offer prospects of putting the disturbing trend of runaway government into reverse. Public expenditure becomes more subject to efficient control when tax-payers are closer to the point at which taxes are spent.

Only one country in the world can be cited where public expenditure at the regional level (the canton) exceeds expenditure by the federal government. That country is Switzerland. Its exceptional way of handling its affairs can be explained on historical and geographical grounds. Communities separated by language and religion and by vast mountains owed little allegiance in earlier times to a central government. Of necessity, decisions had to be taken locally. Federal government provided the framework within which they could associate and pursue common interests. Switzerland is in effect a patchwork of peoples who in other circumstances might have been at each other's throats. Yet the formula for organizing their public affairs has worked so well for Switzerland that it has become a model of stability in a strife-ridden world.

Stability is often the prize of a long period of progress. But progress itself involves discontinuities which lead on to differential selection. Without variation there can be no progressive evolution.

This is where the devolution of power, of financial expenditure and of the programmes that deliver services offer the greatest promise. Variation will occur because people differ in their presumptions, approaches and traditions. And variation of practice will invite comparison. The spotlight will fall equally on the shining example and on the abject failure. People are quick to adopt that which works.

From deprofessionalization to reprofessionalization

Some of the difficult issues that press heavily on society cannot be solved by popular acclamation. They involve complex problems more likely to be understood by the professionals most intimately involved with them. Here domination of the political system, whether by the clapometer or by the conviction politician, has resulted in pushing aside and disregarding professional advice. Teachers and social workers will have their own views on how to deal with indiscipline in class, truancy and delinquency; medical practitioners may consider what system best serves the need to combine limited financial resources with good medical practice; prison officers will possess insights on the type of regime most likely to minimize the risk of prison riots. All too often such voices are not heard until it is too late. Moreover, no radical programme is ever likely to succeed unless it gains the commitment of the operating classes.

Reprofessionalization would entail a change in organizational approach to the management of public affairs. What professional groups need as a worthwhile brief is to be presented with problems that require their views and solutions. In line with those principles recommended for the use of business corporations, professional inputs are needed from concurrent groups rather than from a single commission. Not only does this offer a time-saving over sequentially based organization but professional groups themselves will vary in the character of their inputs. Such variation increases the prospect of striking a richer vein of suggestions. Of course such inputs cannot determine public policy. There is always the risk that professional suggestions may mask some form of vested interests. This is where the principle of concurrent inputs from different groups, whether professional or political, both increases the range of options and offers a measure of protection against any special lobby. Such an elaboration of the organizational system, because it is based on concurrent working parties, does little to delay the moment when a final decision is reached.

These are some of the processes that are likely to displace the way in which political hierarchies operate in the management of public affairs. The pressure to change in the public sector will correspond with the changes coming over the private sector, where effectiveness in the use of resources is far easier to measure.

Once the coming shape of Organization reaches the management of public affairs, the universal nature of modern communications will ensure a rate of learning and of progress without precedent in the history of the world.

13

Forces making for change ——

Nothing changes without reason. For one system to replace another, smoothly and effectively, two conditions are needed in combination: a sense of disillusionment with the old system along with some beckoning model of the new.

That first condition is already near fulfilment. Hierarchical organizations are coming under pressure for one prime reason: what was for long considered their greatest asset, their efficiency, is fast becoming suspect. With its reliance on rules and regulations and with its separation from its operating levels, what has come to pass is that hierarchy has encountered increasing opposition. Not only has the image of a hierarchically driven bureaucracy deepened and hardened in the experience of those who meet it on the outside, but the more significant change is in the eyes of those who have to operate the system. For its essence is that it denies control to those who are capable of meeting their responsibilities. Bureaucracy can be justified only when an administration is served by the incompetent, which at one time doubtless it was.

While reassessment of the efficiency factor is one force making for change, the social factor is another. The increasing numbers of people now educated to think for themselves cannot work comfortably in organizations where as subordinates they have little say over the direction of their efforts. These pressures for change are cultural in origin and owe much to the broad effects of living in a democracy. With no obvious social barriers in sight, ambitions wax among those who have to find their place in the higher ranks of the new meritocracy. This broad advance can be impeded by the omnipotence of the boss and an organization designed to give expression to his personal control.

A third force making for change in a generally well educated society is the gender factor. Power-based hierarchies, with their military overtones, are nearly always dominated by men who create a climate and a style of management into which women do not fit comfortably. Yet there is an approaching paradox here. For while in many countries traditional positions remain unchanged, women are moving into higher education in increasing numbers; and on their graduation they are presenting themselves to the more selective end of the labour market. Talented women are leaving the parental home in search of careers, no longer with the traditional accoutrements of handbags and knitting and travelling in buses, but on planes and trains clutching their personal computers and mobile telephones. Sooner or later, corporations will have to face the problem of whether this source of talent is to be confined to supportive and ancillary roles, or whether gifted women are to enter the managerial core of the firm. In such an event the managerial style and the nature of the organization itself would have to change. Women, and many men too, prefer to work for a firm that they think of as a family or a club or a sports team. Whatever form the organization may take in the mind, it is not one that can be likened to a military operating unit.

Even without any conscious decisions on the fundamentals of Organization, movements are taking place that are largely unseen by outsiders. A counter-culture is infiltrating hierarchy from within to subvert its normal mode of operation. While the hierarchy may be formally respected, it is often disregarded as discreetly as conditions allow. Many of its employees have learned to introduce their own way of doing things. They have discovered the advantages of team-building in the conduct of personal relationships at work. The solidarity of the team provides protection for any dissident sub-culture that develops within the organization. Thereby, the rules and guide-lines generated from a distant top management can be subtly circumvented from time to time wherever it is considered out of touch with realities at the operating level. The hierarchy may appear as strongly entrenched as ever, even while its effective powers are being steadily eroded.

The point has been reached in many business and public sector organizations where teamwork and the command and control system operate side by side without the advantages that either can offer ideally on their own: that means that they can, in effect, work against each other. So the question arises: can this cultural mix continue?

The present position remains unstable. But in the long run it is almost certain to change in a given direction. For while the principles that govern hierarchical management have been refined to the extent that no further development of consequence is likely, teamwork, being still in its formative period, is imperfectly understood.

A conceptual error about teamwork

Teamwork, as the term is used at present, is often a misnomer for collectivist working. A collective refers to a group of people bound together by a common objective and a common style of life and work. For the most part, what they do, they do in unison.

Such an approach can be exemplified in the way in which industry often chooses to tackle problem-solving activities in a group. The project or the problem is broken down into logically-related and successive stages. The members of the group then pool their thoughts in addressing each stage in turn. The significance of individual differences is largely disregarded since the focus falls on the group itself. As a result the same person is liable to dominate at each stage and the voices of potentially valuable contributors may be submerged. That is where, both at the philosophic and practical level, collectivism and individualism are not easily combined.

Collectivist working is especially prominent in cultures where signs of individualism are treated with social disapproval or even as heresies, as in many parts of Asia, including the newly emerging industrial powers. Collectivism survives at some of the highest levels of technological efficiency because it contains many positive features. Buddhism and Shintoism generate a sense of oneness, wholeness, harmony and balance combined with respect for elders. Such deference creates compliance, common values and a fondness for traditional education, much of it founded on rote-memorization. Collectivist working has a particular strength where it can be reconciled with well established organizational structures. A paternalist pattern which can cement common loyalties offers a formula for cooperation, organized progress and continuity of direction. It has undoubtedly contributed to the economic advance of countries along the Asiatic Pacific rim.

What is questionable is whether this formula which combines conformism with collectivism bodes as well for the future as it has served the recent past. Collectivism harnessed by hierarchy is a pattern ill-adapted for coping with the discontinuities of the present world. Recession, downsizing and the unexpected switching of resources from one place to another disrupt long-established social patterns. Conformism and followership begin to lose both their general acceptance and their once conspicuous working advantages. Using the analogy of sport, people may combine with spirit to chase after the same ball in a friendly and relatively unstressed situation. But when the whistle blows and the real game begins, the position changes. The undifferentiated pursuit of a ball is soon exposed as a deficiency in teamwork and a waste of human resources. For a sports team consists not of a group but of a set number of players who combine in contributing their differentiated skills. There is no room for duplication of effort.

The basic principles of teamwork

The introduction of teamwork, in its most advanced form, to industry and business represents a major paradigm shift. The cultural change is no less significant than the change in method and procedure. The hierarchical model, under which each boss oversees a limited number of people, has its origins in military organization. By contrast, teamwork is a concept derived from sport.

Until sport teams became the focus of public attention, teamwork had never entered into industrial vocabulary. An interest in how teams are managed in sport percolated into industry slowly and informally. The principal route was via the after-dinner speaker. The motive behind the invitation to such an obvious outsider in the first instance was to offer light relief from the ardours of long executive working sessions. After the beer comes the story, preferably accompanied by a few funny jokes. Men, in particular, love to follow their own sports team and revel in any local or national success. So it could be a pleasant interlude to listen to yarns about celebrated sporting heroes, about sporting triumphs and how they were accomplished.

The story that evokes rapt attention revolves round the good local or national team that becomes a giant-killer, defeating a team full of superstars. The tale would be best received from the local hero sportsman, but sporting prowess is seldom matched by inspired story-telling and close analytical skills. Instead, the sought-after speaker has become the manager or captain of the team who could explain how it was done.

Human interest can stir the imagination. Amid the unusually relaxed atmosphere the anecdotes would carry the lesson on how an unfancied group of people could achieve so much more than the pundits expected. The principles that underlie the management of any successful sports team are self-evident to the team's manager. But while these were seldom explicitly set out in recounting the history of the team, the message could nonetheless be inferred by the attentive listener.

The first principle is that a good team has to be selected. That principle happens to be out of line with normal practice in most large organizations. In much of industry and the public service a manager is expected to produce a good team from the personnel already in place: poor players cannot be discharged or transferred nor good ones brought in. By contrast, the first priority of the manager of a successful sports team is to ensure that the best players available are brought in to the team, even though this means that others will lose their place.

The second principle relates to the placement of the players. No manager will recruit three goalkeepers. Particular players are right for particular positions. In rugby, front row forwards look physically much the same – squat and thick-set – but in the higher reaches of the sport a fine distinction will be made between the attributes of a tight head prop and a loose head prop. A team is a combination of players with complementary and perfectly matched behavioural skills.

The third principle would appear at first sight to conflict with the second principle with its emphasis on specialization. In fact, the third principle places a requirement on versatility. When a player is appointed to a position on the field the manager does not mark out an area of the turf to which the player will be confined and say: 'When the ball comes into this square area which I have marked with a white line, your job is to kick the ball.' That approach with its narrow definition of territory has its counterpart in employment where it is called a job specification. In sport, by contrast, a player will be given a basic responsibility without there being any hard and fast restrictions on where the player may wander. There will even be occasions when it may be good play for a left wing to cross to the right wing in order to make a tackle. That latitude extended to a player to determine his own boundaries of operation gives rise in turn to the fourth principle.

Principle number four is that a good team contains players who know how to combine well and to base that play on an assessment of the demands of the current situation. Each player needs to take account of what every other player is doing. If, for good reason, one player gets into an unaccustomed position, the other players will be expected to make appropriate adjustments in their own positions.

The fifth principle is that a good team develops its capacity for autonomy on the basis of the strategies and mutual understanding that are fashioned before play begins. On the pitch the players will act with seeming spontaneity. To the onlookers it will scarcely be apparent who is the captain and who the manager or whether those offices exist at all. The understanding between the players has come about because they know each other and have trained together. The manager, who will have played a large part in the prior formulation of the strategy, will have little scope for intervening in operational management once the players are on the field. The analogy, in the case of an industrial company, would be for all the workers to be doing the right thing without anyone appearing to be in charge.

The conflict between team culture and the hierarchy

An organization run on the basis of a traditional hierarchy has its strengths and faults; so also has a team run on collectivist principles. The typical fault of the traditional hierarchy is that the power of decision-making at the top destroys initiative lower down and leads to huge mistakes when things go wrong. The typical fault of the team, when run as a collective, is an inability to face up to an unexpected crisis and to make tough decisions that involve its members.

Historically, these two faults are apt to occur in successive, undulating stages in the life of a company. The Solo Leader whose performance fails to live up to expectations will be displaced by someone keen to make greater use of the abilities of middle management and to cultivate a new style of working. In due course, the new culture is criticized for its drift and weakness. A new seemingly strong Chief Executive is appointed to take over.

Will the pendulum swing to and fro indefinitely? I believe not. The reason is that a deeper understanding of teamwork is developing as people begin to learn its lessons and find ways of relating it to improved overall control allied with greater autonomy in larger organizations.

But learning is not only about effectiveness. An important force making for change is one of personal orientation which arises out of the delayering of organizations. The removal of the prospects of promotion for many means that fewer than ever before will have any reasonable expectation of a lifetime's hold on a job. Individuals will need to think afresh about careers and their career prospects. Like sports people, they may need to move between different teams, as working life progresses, and to find their role in varying situations. As in a sports league a player may leave to join another more senior team and the clubs themselves are arranged to enable this to happen through negotiation.

The Russian doll syndrome

The difference between the sort of organizations to which working people aspire and those to which they are obliged to belong are becoming sharper and more distinct. If one asks the question whether organizations in the field of business and the public service accord with those principles that have proved themselves in the field of sport, the answer must be in the negative. Political systems and business corporations are not run like sports teams.

If any comparisons are to be made on the common characteristics of large organizations irrespective of whether they are operating in the public or private sectors, the most fitting picture is that of Russian dolls.

Wooden Russian dolls are a traditional toy: the outer figure unscrews to reveal an inner figure identical in design to the outer. Likewise, the inner figure unscrews to reveal a smaller figure still. All the dolls fit exactly into their cavities. All are replicas of one another with the very small merely a miniaturized version of the large exterior casing.

Significantly Russian dolls were among the most conspicuous items Russia put on sale in foreign shops during the Stalinist period. Russian dolls symbolize interlocking uniformity. The centralized State is geared to ensure that all its systems are alike. There is no room for deviations. Business corporations often operate along the same lines. Standard systems are accompanied by standard training. As a result they present the same image to the outer world. Many retail chains operate on these lines. The more standardized the product, the more likely it is that the corporation will resemble a set of Russian dolls.

One problem for this particular model is that however well suited it may be to the efficient distribution of a particular product or set of products, the seeds of growth are restricted. The inner dolls are like people unable to escape from their incarceration and too restricted to express their individuality.

Many models serve their function well but have a limited life because they have no development potential. The Russian doll may be locked in on both the inside and the outside. There is no easy way out. That has proved to be the case with some State organizations which, while dynamically defunct, have managed to continue in some parts of the world for several decades at least.

Pressures for change in the public sector

The business corporation and the public service can be compared when they are similar in size. Then they are observed to give rise to similar problems, so offering opportunities for learning from one another. But the question may be asked: will that learning take place?

My contention here is that it will. There will be a transfer of learning from the public sector to the private sector and from the private sector to the public sector. Teamwork is well developed in some areas of the public sector both because of the values held by those who work in the public service and due to the numbers of professionals who work at the same level. But when it comes to innovations in the design of Organization, it is more likely that the private sector will influence the public sector rather than that the influence will work in the reverse direction. The reasons for this belief are fourfold.

The first reason has to do with the greater variety of organizations within the private sector in comparison with the monolithic nature of bodies run by the State. Private sector firms therefore have a greater range of experience and so some will be better placed to capitalize on approaches that can be shown to yield demonstrably superior results.

The second reason is that business corporations learn more rapidly than political entities. That is because business has a clear bottom line. Profits are made or losses are incurred; and if the latter continue, the business collapses. It is a different matter with management in the realm of public affairs. Income is generated by taxation and a country has only one central government. Government in effect runs a monopoly business based on a standardized product. With little diversity there is little scope for evolution. Even within a limited range of experience it is difficult to establish what is learned and what is not.

Rival politicians will be forever proclaiming their different interpretation of the facts and figures.

The third reason relates to accountability, which is faster in the private sector. In the private sector accountability is set by the shareholders' meeting; in the public sector by the electorate. Those responsible for an obsolete approach to management can be ousted in favour of the more progressive and efficient at annual intervals; in the case of the public sector, the event must await a general election that may happen only every four or five years.

The fourth reason for believing that changes in the concept of Organization will move from the private sector to the public sector relates to the transfer of personnel. The monolithic nature of the public sector makes it difficult to innovate in organizational models and in the use of associated techniques. But the public sector is not reluctant to introduce methods whose effectiveness is free from controversy on the grounds that it has been proven elsewhere. The public sector is always willing to hire people who have made their reputations in the private sector but can deliver something of value in the public service. Change will come about as an outgrowth of people developing their consulting businesses or making career moves from the private sector into the public sector.

An increase in the variety of models of Organization would be the biggest factor making for change. Here there are prospects that changes in payment systems could exercise a major influence. The capacity to promote and sustain good teamwork is seldom recognized and is poorly rewarded.

There are at present a great many pressures operating to disturb the design of Organization, which will provide an opportunity to introduce new organizational forms. It is a subject that needs to be kept permanently under review. And as new models are discussed and tried out experimentally, there will be a new surge of interest, learning and progress.

14

The evolution of common shape ────────────

All human society is based on the division of labour. The problem of contemporary society is to establish the principle upon which that division of labour should be based and whether there is now scope for some move in a progressive direction.

Throughout the history of the human race, the issue of how work is organized has always been important but has seldom been debated. As a rule tradition ensures that roles in life are taken for granted. In a hunting and gathering society, the division of work was based on sex. Men did the hunting, women the gathering. There was an associated set of duties and responsibilities that sprang from that primary division, with sex always operating as the dividing point. Men never did women's work and women never did men's work.

A secondary form of organization was age-related. That was why initiation ceremonies played such an important part. As people (mainly males) passed from one critical age group to the next, physical markings and often violent ceremonies would convey the change in roles and privileges that were brought about.

The hunting and gathering society would seldom comprise more than one hundred members. Once that number was exceeded, a smaller group would break away from the larger group and go off in search of another territory. In the case of the larger groups, some basis of authority or decision-making was needed. An anthropological survey of such groups makes plain the range of formulae available. Some groups were communistic in their living and consensus-oriented in their decision-making; some were ruled by male elders, some by a hereditary monarch who sounded out tribal feeling before arriving at pronouncements; others were subject to personal power wielded by a chief.

It is almost certain that it was the last of these forms that brought about the next stage in the evolution of Organization. Personal power can both limit scope and create expanding opportunity. The former occurs where power is exercised but never shared. It is commonly exemplified in small businesses today where people refer to 'the big fish in the small pond'. Everything revolves around one dominant person. I have known many small businesses where its owner in effect declares: 'I don't wish to expand my business to a point where I would lose personal control. I enjoy it as it is.'

Big fish, bigger pond

When groups expand beyond the magic figure of one hundred, to the point where it is no longer possible for everyone to know everyone, something radical has to change. The one person cannot personally control everything. Yet, paradoxically, everything can be subject to the whims and control of a single person. That possibility arises when the dominant figure feels such confidence in the loyalty of a few obsequious supporters that some element of power can be passed on to them in the full knowledge that it can always be taken back again. The appointment of lieutenants is a big organizational step forward. Once the formula is adopted, the road is set for expansion. The formal organization chart begins. Provided personal allegiance can be retained by whoever wields the power, small empires can grow into big empires. What made for competitive advantage in the evolutionary contest of organizations on the world scene was not so much their economies of scale, with which mass production is associated, as the scale of their economies.

Early empires first introduced major irrigation systems. Buildings designed for the safe storage of crops provided security against the vagaries of the seasons, so releasing labour that would otherwise have been engaged in the struggle for subsistence. Landing places became harbours. Fishing boats for local use became sea-going vessels bringing back commercial goods from distant places. Collections of documents, first used for trade, grew into libraries. Places of traditional teaching became schools and centres of learning. Local shrines grew into temples and cathedrals. Habitations became fortresses and places from which expansion and conquest were planned. Tight, disciplined organizations swept all before them. Like has competed with like in variants of a single organizational pattern. Throughout the greater part of history the formula has remained much the same.

In previous chapters I have outlined the imperfections to which traditional hierarchy has become eventually subject as a form of Organization. Its displacement is not, however, easily brought about. Hierarchy is based on power. Countries with a strong political power base may become tyrannies. Hence tyrants who feel threatened react

Models of organization according to size

Experience suggests that small organizations can still function well based on the 'big fish in a small pond', even though this presents eventual problems for growth and for management succession. An intermediate size of organization creates opportunity for a 'command and control' hierarchy, which can operate satisfactorily until it becomes undermined by sluggishness and bureaucracy. Interacting teamwork best serves the complexities of the larger organization. In very large organizations, especially those that are multi-ethnic, political factors assume an overriding importance. Failure to address the issue means that minorities are liable to be permanently deprived of their natural democratic rights or feel discriminated against. Here consociation or some form of voluntary affirmative action can redress the balance.

UP TO 100   **UP TO 400**

400 PLUS   **A MILLION PLUS**

by increasing their tyranny. The overthrow of tyrants and the regimes they have set in place is often prolonged and bloody and is not even inevitable. In that sense evolution moves slowly.

In this respect the world of the business corporation provides a contrast. The evolution of Organization in the business world is better placed to proceed more rapidly, for business tycoons are more easily displaced than political tyrants. Profits are made or losses are incurred; and if the latter continue, business collapses. He who stands at the helm is both accountable and vulnerable. That process provides a mighty stimulus to learning.

It is a different matter with management in the realm of public affairs. Income is generated by taxation and a country has only one central government. Government in effect runs a monopoly business based on a standardized product. With little diversity there is little scope for evolution. Even within a limited range of experience it is difficult to establish what is learned and what is not. Rival politicians will be forever proclaiming their different interpretations of the facts and figures.

In the business world the impetus of competition is throwing up variants in pattern as one Chief Executive replaces another and endeavours to satisfy the expectations of the various stakeholders. Yet patterns are changing slowly rather than dramatically. For one thing, managers brought up in the current school of thinking about the nature of management and what they consider is fitting for leadership from the front are unlikely to revise their thoughts radically in some new direction. But they do so, only occasionally. Revisionist thinking is usually prompted by a crisis and takes the form of a reaction against the style of leadership of an ill-fated predecessor.

Three systems for the future

I have earlier drawn attention to the different types of team that are needed to run a complex corporation, whether in the private or public sector, and to the different types of abilities that naturally come to the fore in these different teams. One can establish the need for strategic teams and operational teams and cross-functional teams that handle liaison and information issues. So-called autonomous work groups have already come into their own.

Yet there are dangers in this process. The dismantling of hierarchy can quickly lead to the formation of inward-looking and self-regarding groups. Group meetings can soon resemble talk shops. With the loss of authority the ability to integrate the work of groups in adjacent fields is liable to be lost as is the capacity to handle large-scale complex projects.

Group work and team work are styles of working; they do not in themselves constitute a form of Organization. The merit of hierarchy is that it offers a command system and a mechanism for decision-taking. Hierarchy cannot be safely dismantled unless the core of what makes it effective can be retained in some way.

If the objective is to combine a team approach with an overall effective organization, three approaches are now to be seen on the agenda of the corporation.

Cultivating the team leader

The first system focuses on the development of the team leader along with some increased awareness of the expectations of team members themselves. Teamwork is established within the framework of the current hierarchy and without disturbance to the basic system of organization. The team leader is responsible for forming the team, for conducting its operations and for liaising with the rest of the organization on the matter of both its inputs and its outputs. It is held that all executives can be trained for team leadership for which well established forms of training are now available.

The logic of this approach is commendable. But in practice the focus of emphasis on the team leader is prone to downgrade the position of the team members. The so-called team soon becomes in effect a group whose members lack any conspicuous individuality. Even the leadership issue can falter. The casting of the most senior person as the team leader is often automatic and is therefore in large part a cosmetic operation. The titular team leader does not behave like a team player and after a while, and in spite of the training received, reverts to a display of those strengths and styles of behaviour that have been exhibited and appreciated in a different context. That is why it is such a common experience to hear how someone who is indisputably an achiever often turns into a poor team leader. When that happens the traditional strengths and weaknesses of the hierarchy remain largely as they were. Nothing really has changed other than the way in which the organization chooses to describe itself.

A system of team hierarchies

The second system is based on a hierarchy of teams with the prime responsibility being placed on the team rather than on any particular individual. The teams then decide on how roles should be distributed between the members. This is a system that facilitates what is termed situational leadership or rotating leadership, theoretical possibilities that best come to life when individuals have recognized team roles. Command and control, the strong point of hierarchy, can be retained by the organizational structure. Teams are ranked in position according to team seniority. The strategic group constitutes the top management, while the operational management is made up of middle managers.

A system of organization based on team structures makes for greater devolution of responsibility, less interference on the part of one level on another and better integration of effort on the part of individuals working at the same level.

Whatever the merits of this approach, viewed from the angle of the team, the system does not lend itself well to career development and to the expectations that go with seniority and length of service. Effective operational managers expect recognition and that this will be rewarded in terms of promotion and salary. There would be pressure to turn good operational managers into poor strategic managers in order to reward their seniority, so offering another instance of 'promotion to a level of incompetence'. That possibility becomes a real danger because movement in a given direction is the only form of career development available. The resulting problems may end up close to those prevailing in organizations at the present day.

A system of interacting circles

A third, and more radical, approach to the reform of organizations is to dispense with hierarchy, which by its nature focuses on promotion by age and length of service, entry into dead men's shoes and the awaiting of 'Buggins' turn'. The attraction of a seniority-based system of hierarchy to those on the inside is that it is presumed to protect jobs, salaries and rank. The possibility that it is liable to be counter-productive has been overlooked. A system that leads to overpromotion and overpayment generates its own syndrome of problems. Middle-aged executives are especially subject to 'early retirement' during cutbacks, even at the peak of their physical and mental fitness. Once back on the labour market, they become victims of prejudicial age discrimination when job-seeking. People in senior positions are often very defensive in the way in which they conduct themselves and are very wary of anything to do with organizational change. That resistance is hardly surprising.

This state of affairs can be radically altered in an organization where people move regularly between different positions and between different teams and where no-one has a permanent claim or hold on a particular job. Such an organization allows an internal labour market to be set up based on comprehensive and continuous assessment, to which all would contribute and to which all would be subject. Remuneration could then depend on team performance with individuals enjoying a supplementary bonus based on the level of demand for entry into a team. Teams would bid for particular members to join them, naturally being attracted to those known to be most effective in their role. Under such conditions people have the best chance of finding themselves engaged in positions to which they are suited. No working person is liable to be as overpriced or overpromoted as in a hierarchy.

Dispensing with hierarchy has implications not only for the position of individuals but also for the position of teams within the organization. A strategic team with a broader orbit of responsibility than an operational team implies that its members would enjoy seniority and higher salaries. Certainly the work involved in these teams calls for different skills but that is not to say that one skill is inherently superior to the other. Differences in levels of skill and experience can be expected within each type of team and will be reflected in the demand for the services of particular individuals to join the respective teams. The separation of the function of the team from the seniority issue allows relatively junior members who possess suitable aptitudes to join strategic teams. There they can gain invaluable experience at an early age and be assessed further in relation to their potential. Conversely, a senior member of a corporation who possesses valuable operational skills that belong ideally to an operational team might well encumber the workings of a strategic team. Automatic entry into such a team can debilitate the effectiveness of organizations.

A strategic team needs in its strategic deliberations members with immediate operational experience; otherwise, its conclusions will betray some failure to take account of practical realities. That being so, there will be a number of candidates with operational experience who could make up the team. The choice depends very much on the balance of team roles between the current team members together with the calibre of the possible candidates. That is why personnel selection in internal career movement is so important, both for adding strength to the team and for avoiding damage to the team balance that is the common consequence of ex officio entry.

I have chosen to describe this pattern of recommended Organization as one of interacting circles. Visually the movements of its members are as difficult to track as those moving within a honey bee's nest or a termite mound: there is no allotted territory within which the individual is confined. In a developing, and fast moving, human organization membership of teams can overlap. At the same time different strategic teams can also act concurrently and are empowered to make decisions that fall within their orbit. There is no longer a need to wait until certain senior figures make themselves available.

This pattern of Organization has much to offer once numbers within a firm or corporation climb to 400 or more but there is also some limited evidence that it can hold good with somewhat smaller numbers. A crucial factor in all this is the level of sophistication and culture of the members. That level needs to be generally high if the pattern is to prove viable and advantageous.

The progression helix

Management organization and career progression can be represented on a common chart expressed as a continuous upward process. Recruits enter at different points and in particular positions. They move forward as they prove their worth by their contribution to the teams. The excellence of their contribution affects seniority. Contribution becomes a more significant pointer to progression than whether executives are primarily engaged on strategic, professional or operational activities.

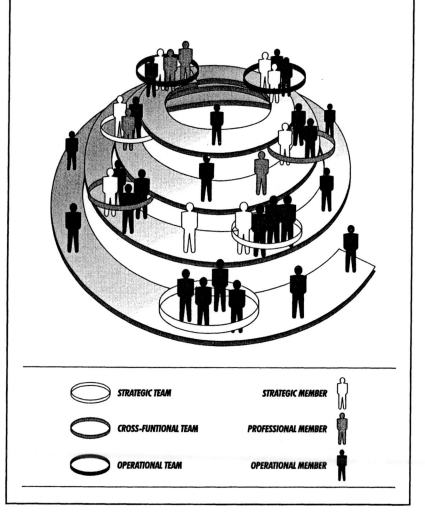

STRATEGIC TEAM	STRATEGIC MEMBER
CROSS-FUNTIONAL TEAM	PROFESSIONAL MEMBER
OPERATIONAL TEAM	OPERATIONAL MEMBER

There is a risk that interacting teams and circles can generate an element of confusion. That is why an element of hierarchy needs to be retained, for the scope and challenge of some teams will be greater than that of others. Those who succeed at one level will spiral upwards to bigger challenges, for these interacting circles are not amorphous in their overall formation but can be likened to a helix.

All the elements I have described in this third pattern, although not the model itself, are already in existence. A small number of corporations have taken steps in this direction and are conscious of living through a period of revolutionary change. But other things remain as they were. What has not as yet happened is any shift in the general system of remuneration. Until that happens organizations will have a hybrid character, belonging neither to traditional hierarchy nor to the pattern of interacting circles. This will create a climate of uncertainty about the direction in which things are moving, for people will remain uncertain as to whether they should strive for individual recognition or for their contribution to group achievement – and that uncertainty will affect their performance.

An association of peoples

The principles of Organization change as size increases. The big fish in the small pond can work well with the smallest entrepreneurial and social entities, while at the other end of the scale, a new set of factors come into play as political considerations outweigh the economic. This is an area in which human organizations have had very little success.

Here large multinational corporations experience problems not unlike those besetting the multicultural Nation State. The essence of the problem is that whatever the rulers decide is unacceptable to one, or some, of the less powerful or numerically smaller groups. Bigness now works against stability.

In private sector corporations there has been a sudden growth of interest in cross-cultural communication. The immediate reason for this is that head offices in a metropolitan area develop concern that plans developed centrally are not being received as they should by outlying establishments in foreign countries. This is held to be partly a language problem and partly a problem about how to approach matters in a way that is acceptable to the local culture.

There is, however, a deeper issue that is overlooked. It is not that the corporation needs better trained missionaries but that the missionary approach will not serve the interests of the multinational in the long run. People do not accept change unless they become part of the process. That entails some substantial dismantling of head office bureaucracy and some relinquishment of centralized power.

That realization accounts for the beginnings of a transformation of multinationals into transnationals. Transnationals started not as a conscious form of organizational improvement but as a response to nationalistic governments that demanded the presence of nationals on the boards of inward-investing companies in return for concessions including those of tax. The early experience of transnationals then began to show some spin-off advantages. Firms in which locals with a very different background from that of metropolitan executives play a significant part in decision-making have a much greater measure of stability. Multinationals often pay great attention to those cultural factors that affect manners, behaviour and conventions. But the more abiding problem relates to the way in which the locals have to come to terms with foreigners, rising above differences to create some unique combined order of their own.

The analogy is close to the problems of Empire or of the large Nation State. The Empire holds for a time while there is something to hold it together. But after that, when the dynamism is lost, it is inescapable that there will be disaffected provinces. At their best, they prove troublesome; at their worst, they become separatist and even fanatical in their separatism. Traditional democracy offers no solution here because the majority overwhelms the minority.

The potential solution for organizations is no different in principle from that provided by the policy of developing interacting circles. Those who are part of the whole need to be represented in the whole. If the words of the poet are true that 'no man is an island', no community or group of peoples can be sustained in an island either. Some form of belongingness has to be created which is not based simply on a head-count.

Such a form has been proposed by the concept of consociation, a word first coined by Lijphart, a Dutch sociologist who lived in Canada and worked for part of his life in South Africa. Lijphart observed that rival groups could live in relative harmony when they participated in government as of right and that this could be brought about by appropriate constitutional structures. Holland and Malaysia, and more especially Switzerland, have many of the characteristics of a consociation. There is a scoffing jest that no-one can think of a famous Swiss personality other than William Tell. Yet when the coin is turned to the other side, a compliment is revealed. Switzerland has no Solo Leaders and never has had. For Switzerland is essentially a federation in which cantons and communes agree to pass on some of their powers to the centre. The centre is respected for it is unable to dominate. And if it is to influence, it has to persuade.

It is a matter of speculation as to how far the ideas of Lijphart were embodied in the constitution of the new South Africa. All groups that poll over three per cent of the electoral vote have a right to participate in government. However, the President chooses which individuals from these various groups will be invited to hold governmental posts. The principle therefore is that of an organization combining representation with selection.

Representation plus selection offers an important organizational distinction from representation without selection. Without the operation of an effective selection factor individuals might find themselves locked in incompatible partnerships, as often happens when strong leaders of parties and factions confront each other. In the framework of a consociation priorities change: communities need leaders who can work with leaders of other communities. There is a change, too, in the attitudes of the rank and file when some of the factors that characterize a consociation are present. People canvas for the fulfilment of their aims rather than for the defeat of the other side. In terms of South Africa itself I had occasion to work there briefly both under the old regime and under the new. Nothing impressed me more than the shift in the position of those previously subject to the pull of extremism. A new scenario created new attitudes. One cannot expect attitudes to change in the long run until organizations are created that provide the climate for cooperation.

A next step in human evolution

Organization has been at the centre of the evolution of the human species. Personal power was needed to bring about the first large-scale accomplishments that mark the dawn of civilization. Much of human history has been taken up with the exercise of that power and of the consequences that arose when various power groups clashed. The importance of Organization has been much neglected, perhaps because not many varieties of it are to be found throughout much of human history.

The nature of Organization, on the evidence of what has happened in history, has a direct bearing on what will eventuate. With its distinct traditions and rules it defines our identity, tells us who are our friends and who are our enemies. It has the power to demand from us sacrifice. Many have given their lives willingly for the Organization. The concept of biologically rooted 'social donorism', first identified by biologists in the higher termites, would seem equally applicable to us. Its powerful force is pressing for expression. If frustrated it can lead to destructive displacement activities. The readiness to make sacrifices, including the supreme sacrifice on behalf of the 'community', begs the questions of how we recognize which community it is to which we belong. Once the sacrifice denotes fighting and killing others, as it often does, it becomes a serious matter.

If 'social donorism' can be more widely recognized, it can be developed to have a wider and more positive significance in the world around us. It is already to be found in the community concept of management, as contained in the African word 'Ubuntu'. One Zulu phrase captures more specifically the balance between individualism and collectivism. The expression: 'Umuntu Ngumintu Ngabantu' freely translated means; 'I am because you are; you are because we are'.

It is for such a reason that education together and the development of careers need to move us forward in a coordinated way so that we can become accepted members of other groups. We can only do so when we have a role to play. That role has to be discovered in one group and transferred to another, which for technological reasons can now happen more easily than ever before.

Human evolution once centred on physical characteristics. A brain capable of advanced intelligence, refined speech leading to intricate forms of communication and manipulative hands that could fashion precision tools – all these produced competitive advantage. That era is drawing to a close. Another is beginning. It is now social and organizational development which will determine human success or failure during the twenty-first century along a route down which we must now evolve.

Epilogue ———————————————————

The material collected for this book was prompted by my experience and observations that teamwork in business and the public services was being hampered by bureaucracy. Bureaucracy I assessed to be an outgrowth of multilevel hierarchy and I have been in accord with the mood of the times in supporting the delayering of hierarchies. That is why I favoured something I now see as being too simplistic, the creation of a two-level hierarchy, separating the strategic and operational functions.

After further studies, what this book has proposed is that we need something more radical still, if businesses and institutions are to progress in a more dynamic direction. The nature of Organization, especially that which is based on a single line of control, determines the character of what is encompassed, irrespective of the professed values and the capabilities of the reputed leader. It is the reason why authoritarian multilevel hierarchies end up with much the same behaviour patterns. An inner corrosion eventually undermines whatever progress may formerly have been achieved.

Both stability and dynamism occur when all sub-systems of Organization contribute to and interact with one another in an integrated way and it is here that the higher insects score over humans.

Management has been described by a leading management theorist, Kotter, as a 'capacity for coping with complexity' and in that sense and under their specific conditions the higher insects appear to be superior managers with their evident advantage springing from good self-management contained within the various sub-systems of the colony. The stability of the process depends on contributions from different 'castes' of individual and is achieved by creating a population balance between the range of specialized 'castes'. In such a way perfect teamwork is built up. Much human teamwork, as it may be called, pays no attention to 'caste' differentiation; instead group-think and leader dominance create undifferentiated conformism.

In contrast to the definition of management, Kotter describes leadership as 'a capacity for coping with change'. In this area the higher insects cannot compete with humans, for change demands vision and the capacity to innovate and to communicate in a way that can wrest others from existing habits and attitudes. This cluster of attributes is uniquely human but unevenly distributed. Being a multifaceted activity, it often needs the skills and personal qualities of different individuals. People can share in the leadership function and it is desirable that they should do so, for otherwise dependence in such a critical function on one possibly fallible person, however talented, puts at risk the stability of the total system. Yet because of the wide-ranging scope of its outputs the proportion of those engaged in this function must inevitably be small in relation to the size of the enterprise or the public body. The selection of 'caste' members is critical. That is why leadership always appears a minority function, élitist in its operations and prone to become isolated. It is a danger that has to be countered. The remedy is to encourage the free movement of individuals between teams that are empowered to take on and discharge responsibility. Such a process, properly monitored, provides the means of selecting individuals in an upwards spiral for further positions within the total system.

The relationship of levels in human hierarchies has so far been simple and two-dimensional, whereas the organization of integrated activities among the higher insects is three-dimensional, socially complex and fostered on a system of multimodal communications. Their senses equip them to live in a world to which the human mind is far removed. But this gap in these respective capacities can now be bridged by the way in which computers have enhanced our ability to communicate with our fellows in a way that would have been unimaginable a few decades ago.

I have reached the conclusion that higher forms of Organization lie within our reach. Ultimately they will combine the devolved but integrated strengths of the higher insects with the directive and strategic abilities of humans. The model will take the form of a helix, allowing for continuous upward rotation. My confidence that this will happen is founded on a belief in the forward movement of the designs that underlie evolution; and, further, that once new and superior models of Organization begin to appear the advance will gather pace as the subject gains the attention of management. So fast will it move that the future may look almost as monolithic as the present in the character of Organization. But that character will be quite different from that with which we are familiar.

For the moment we should encourage and value diversity in design of Organization. We should attach more importance to a system that offers the best prospects for combining growth with stability than to one which places its prime emphasis on the selection of bosses with commanding talents or an appealing charisma. Here, any conflict in priorities may be short-lived. Any newly devised system will ultimately bring forth leaders in its own image and create a new set of expectations among the public. A new generation of outstanding men and women will arise, better able to work together than their forebears, and more attuned to the shape of society emerging in the new millennium.

Appendix 1

Exercises

The aim of these exercises is to create an increased interest in Organization and on the way in which it affects all aspects of working activity.

Exercise 1 was developed recently by the author as a means of throwing light on the trend in industry to replace single-strand work with mixed work, where work is described as 'a bit of this, a bit of that and a bit of the other'. Single-strand work has tended to disappear through becoming either automated or outsourced. This latter work-type, being a more adaptable adjustment, tended to survive but its downside has been found to be work-drift: a gap would open up between what a worker actually did and was officially supposed to be doing. On the debit side, individuals might neglect those parts of mixed work that did not appeal, or, on the positive side, would respond constructively to demands of the work situation outside the original job specification. In these circumstances a key to efficient management was found to lie in the relationship between the briefing given to the worker and the way in which that briefing is interpreted. These studies have resulted in a computer-based means of assigning and monitoring work, called Workset. Among its outputs, Workset will present an instantly available analysis of the working culture of an organization. A fully developed and field tested product will be available in 1997.

Exercise 2 first alerted the author in a practical way to the vacuity of buzzwords in management. Teamwork has become an almost conventional image projected by many large firms. So it seemed a useful inquiry to check on how far this mode of working actually affected decision making. Our results did not show a good fit between the observed 'culture' of an organization and the claims it made about itself. But this inquiry was carried out on only a small scale and needs to be repeated before any broad conclusions can be reached.

Exercise 1

Students should be asked to examine a job they know well and to break down its demands into four categories.

The first should be *core tasks*. These refer to predictable and recurring types of work assigned to an individual to be carried out in a set way in order to meet standards of quality, safety or efficiency.

The second should be *peripheral tasks*. This category refers to necessary work assigned to an individual to be carried out at that individual's discretion.

The third category relates to *individual responsibility*. Here the individual is given goals that have to be met but the nature of the tasks necessary to meet those goals is not laid down.

The fourth category refers to *team responsibility*. Here goals and tasks are shared between several people who have to decide between them how the work is to be performed and who does what.

The student should estimate what proportion of time is spent in each category and what is likely to happen if these proportions were to change. Variants of the exercise include comparing the patterns formed by different jobs and, where students come from different establishments, how these patterns compare, whether they relate to the nature of work carried out in these various establishments or reflect the attitudes of management on how work should be distributed. Further, students should assess the preferred mix of work as it would apply to their own ideal jobs. Differences between the preferences of individuals should be discussed in terms of the type of work to which a person is best suited. In that context the case of misfits should be brought up. The question should be posed as to whether particular cases are likely to be general misfits or whether an alleged misfit might fit quite well in a job that offered a different pattern of demands.

The teacher should attempt to build on the significance of the way in which work is set up as a background to the many problems that can arise.

Exercise 2

This exercise explores the prevalence of general cultural patterns. Students should be asked to examine the relationship between teamworking and decision-making in the work areas with which they are familiar. Two ratings are required on the scale of one to ten.

The first rating relates to the prevalence of teamwork in the organization and can be assessed by the proportion of time spent in internal interpersonal communication, in work sharing and in helping one another. If all work were carried out individually, the rating would be one; if all work were shared, the rating would be ten.

The second rating relates to the use of decisions or views reached by the group in their area of competence. Is the group empowered to act on those decisions or do they need ratification by another body? Total absence of empowerment would receive a rating of one and full empowerment a rating of ten. A rider to this exercise involves an estimate of the time needed for external ratification where the group is not empowered to act on its own internal working decisions.

The results of the first rating should now be compared with the results of the second rating. Are individuals working in teams more empowered than those working on their own? The teacher can bring out the dangers of teamwork without empowerment in terms of fuzziness. A low rating on both scales can be indicative of an uncoordinated bureaucracy.

The object of this second exercise is to discuss what constitutes the ideal balance and what external factors can change the balance.

Appendix 2

The nine team roles ———————

The nine team roles originally described in *Team Roles at Work* are as follows:

Roles and descriptions – team-role contribution	Allowable weaknesses
Plant: Creative, imaginative, unorthodox. Solves difficult problems.	Ignores details. Too preoccupied to communicate effectively.
Resource investigator: Extrovert, enthusiastic, communicative. Explores opportunities. Develops contacts.	Overoptimistic. Loses interest once initial enthusiasm has passed.
Co-ordinator: Mature, confident, a good chairperson. Clarifies goals, promotes decision-making, delegates well.	Can be seen as manipulative. Delegates personal work.
Shaper: Challenging, dynamic, thrives on pressure. Has the drive and courage to overcome obstacles.	Can provoke others. Hurts people's feelings.
Monitor evaluator: Sober, strategic and discerning. Sees all options. Judges accurately.	Lacks drive and ability to inspire others. Overly critical.
Teamworker: Co-operative, mild, perceptive and diplomatic. Listens, builds, averts friction, calms the waters.	Indecisive in crunch situations. Can be easily influenced.
Implementer: Disciplined, reliable, conservative and efficient. Turns ideas into practical actions.	Somewhat inflexible. Slow to respond to new possibilities.
Completer: Painstaking, conscientious, anxious. Searches out errors and omissions. Delivers on time.	Inclined to worry unduly. Reluctant to delegate. Can be a nit-picker.
Specialist: Single-minded, self-starting, dedicated. Provides knowledge and skills in rare supply.	Contributes on only a narrow front. Dwells on technicalities. Overlooks the 'big picture'.

Strength of contribution in any one of the roles is commonly associated with particular weaknesses. These are called allowable weaknesses. Executives are seldom strong in all nine team roles.

Further reading

Alexander, R. (1989) Evolution of the Human Psyche. In P. Mellors and C. Stringer (eds) *The Human Revolution*, Edinburgh University Press.

Bridges, W. (1995) *Jobshift: How to Prosper in a Workplace without Jobs*, Allen & Unwin, London.

Christie, P., Lessem, R. and Mbigi, L. (eds) (1994) *African Management*, Knowledge Resources, Randburg, South Africa.

Darlington, C. D. (1969) *The Evolution of Man and Society*, Allen & Unwin, London.

Dimock, M. E. (1960) *Administrative Vitality: The Conflict with Bureaucracy*, Routledge and Kegan Paul, London.

Etzioni, A. (1993) *The Spirit of Community*, Crown, New York.

Free, J. B. (1993) *The Social Organization of Honey Bees*, Northern Bee Books, Hebden Bridge.

von Frisch, K. (1954) *The Dancing Bees: An Account of the Life and Senses of the Honey Bee*, Methuen, London.

Garrett, B. (1992) Creating The Culture of the Learning Organization: The Challenge for Learning Leaders. In M. Syrett and C. Hogg (eds), *Frontiers of Leadership*, Blackwell, Oxford.

Hampden-Turner, C. and Trompenaars, A. (1994) *The Seven Cultures of Capitalism*, Piatkus, London.

Jewkes, J. *et al.* (1969) *The Sources of Invention*, 2nd edition, Macmillan, London.

Koopman, A. (1991) *Transcultural Management*, Blackwell, Oxford.

Lijphart, A. (1975) *The Politics of Accommodation*, Berkeley, California.

Lodge, G. C. (1995) *Managing Globalization in the Age of Interdependence*, Pfeiffer, San Diego.

Semler, R. (1993) *Maverick: The Success Story Behind The World's Most Unusual Workplace*, Arrow, London.

Syrett, M. and Hogg, C. (eds) (1992) *Frontiers of Leadership*, Blackwell, Oxford.

Wilson, E. O. (1971) *The Insect Societies*, Harvard University Press. See especially Chapter 17, The Genetic Theory of Social Behaviour.

Zuboff, S. (1988) *In the Age of the Smart Machine: the Future of Work and Power*, Butterworth-Heinemann, Oxford.

Index ————————————

Alpha male dominance, 85, 87
Altruistic behaviour, 31
Ants, 55
  organization behaviour, 26
Astrology, guide to the future, 2
Astronomy, guide to the future, 2
Attention limits, 19, 21
Authoritarian culture, 73
Autocracies, tyrannical, 85

Bees, 55
  organization behaviour, 24–6
Bottlenecks, see Single channel
  capacity
Branson, Richard, 5
Bribe culture, 73
Budget spending pattern, 9
Bureaucratic behaviour, 9–11, 116

Capital purchases policy, 10
Career development, 51–2, 58, 59,
  61–2
  high-order talent, 67–8
  internal transfers, 81–2
Castes:
  in insect behaviour, 27, 30
  in management, 32, 116, 117
Casting Director, 58–60
Chance factors, effect on business,
  79–80

China, market liberalism, 2
Civilizations, history, 4, 24
Clapometer, 87
Collective security needs, 93
Collectivist working, 97–8
Command and control model, 12,
  13, 106
  parallel operation, 97
Communication, cross-cultural, 71–2,
  112
Communications problems, 71–3,
  112
Communications technology, 5
Competition, in ideas, 35
Competitive advantage, 4–5
Concurrent operating, 36, 38, 39, 40
Consensus culture, 73
Consociation, 113
Consultants, self-employed, 82
Core tasks, 120
Corporations:
  behaviour, 8–9
  culture, see Culture
  leadership image, 22
  multinational, 73–4, 112
  transnational, 74, 113
Cross-functional teams, 46, 47
Culture, 45, 70, 120
  changes, 74, 76
  corporation, 71–2
  multinationals, 73–4
  resolving problems, 72–3
  types, 73

Decision-making process:
  exercise, 120–1
  types, 37
Delayering, 12, 15, 89
Democracy, 85
Devolution, 89–90
  government powers, 92–4
Differential survival, 4
Division of labour, 4, 28, 54
  managerial, 79
  traditional basis, 104
Downsizing, 12, 89

Education, use of teamwork, 52–3
Efficiency factor, force for change, 96
Election principle, 90–2
Empire state, 113
Employment services,
  de-professionalization, 1
Eusocial insects, 29, 30–1, *see also*
  Ants; Bees; Termites
Evolution, management, 4–6, 114–15

Falklands War, decision-making
  example, 19
Financial control strategies, 12–13
Fish stock control example, 88
Followership, 14–15
Forecasting accuracy, 3
Function (definition), 44

Gender factor, force for change, 96–7
Government role:
  devolution of power, 90, 92
  exercise of power, 84–5, 86–7
  local, 86, 92–3
  monopoly business, 107
Group sizing, 36

'Head hunters', 13
Health field:
  costs study, 89
  use of teamwork, 53

Hierarchical decision-making, 14–15,
  16–17, 34, 41
  changes in, 96–7
  faults, 100–1
  merits, 108
Horizontality concept, 34
Hospitals, *see* Health field

Impulsive behaviour, 33–4
Incentive schemes, 49
Individual responsibility, 120
Industrial training schemes, 88–9
Intelligence, superior use, 28
Inter-acting circles model, 106,
  109–10
Interplace (human resource
  management system), 9, 42
Inventiveness, 64–5

Job Clubs, 1
Job (definition), 44
Job specifications, 49–50

Kinship culture, 73

Leadership, 117
  ideal types, 46, 47
  importance, 22
  personal characteristics, 14–15
  and teamwork, 16–17
  working styles, 17–18
Lijphart, A., 113
Local government role, 86, 92–3

Magistrates selection procedure,
  91–2
Management, definition, 116
Market changes, effect on business,
  80
'Maxwell Factor', 5

Maxwell, Robert, 5
Multi-tiered hierarchy, *see*
    Organizations, multi-tiered
Multinational corporations, *see*
    Corporations, multinational

Nation state, 113
Nervous system, human, 19, 20
Non-executive directors, 81

Operational management, 43, 77, 79
Operational teams, 46, 47
Organizations:
    ailing, 33
    coping with highly-talented
        people, 66–9
    future patterns, 107–12, 116–18
    human achievements, 85
    multi-tiered, 17, 41
    non-hierarchical, 41
    sizing, 23, 105–6, 112

Party conference, policy making, 87
Passive approach, 2–3
Pay differentials, 16
Peripheral tasks, 120
Personal power, 104–5
Placement within team, 99
Political control approach, 87
Predestination belief, 2
Proactive approach, 2–3
Producer systems, evolution, 4
Progression helix, 111
Public service sector:
    changes needed, 102–3
    decision-making, 86–7
    organization, 6–7, 107
    see also under Government role

Quality Calamity exercise, 38

Redundancies, effect, 12
Representation plus selection
    process, 114
Reprofessionalization, 94–5
Research and development projects,
    stages, 56–7

Responsibility:
    fragmentation, 50–1
    individual, 120
Revisionist thinking, 107
Russian doll syndrome, 101–2

Salary levels, top, 15
Schools, *see* Education
Second World War, decision-making
    example, 21
Selection principle, 90–2, 99
Self-sacrifice, *see* Altruistic behaviour
'Selfish gene', 31
Single channel capacity, 20, 21
'Social donorism', 31, 114
Social factor, force for change, 96
Solo leaders, 18, 100
South African constitution, 113–14
Specialization, 44, 99–100
Standardization, government
    programmes, 86
Strategic management, 43, 77–8, 79,
    82–3
Strategic teams, 46, 47, 80–1
    filling gaps, 81–2
Structured work, 54
Subordinates, reporting by, 11–12
Succession planning, 33–4
Sweden, unemployment, 2
Switzerland, public affairs
    administration, 94
Systems of beliefs, 75–6

Talented people:
    career development, 67–8
    high-order, 64–7
Team empowerment, 39, 51, 54
Team leader, 108
Team responsibility, 120
Teams:
    and career development, 61–2
    change opportunities, 57–8
    development opportunities, 60–1
    hierarchy, 108–9
    inter-company communications,
        62
    social responsibilities, 62
    strategic, *see* Strategic teams

Teamwork, 13, 16–17, 44–5
  concurrent operation, 36, 38, 39, 40
  in education, 52–3
  exercise, 120–1
  faults, 100–1
  in health field, 53
  parallel operation, 97
  principles, 98–100
Tempo, working, 21
Termites, organization behaviour, 27
Thatcherism strategy, 1
Total Quality Control, 78

Transnational corporations, *see* Corporations, transnational
Trapezium Organization model, 6, 42–3
  distortions, 43–4

Unemployment benefit payments, 89, 93
Unstructured work, 54

Work groups, autonomous, 107, 108
Workset (work monitoring programme), 119

INTERPLACE
BELBIN Team Role Expert System

INTERPLACE takes the original Team Role concepts dealt with in Dr. Belbin's original book, *Management Teams: Why they Succeed or Fail*, and transforms all information-input into a compatible and quickly understandable language.

INTERPLACE can deal with three types of input:
*   how in team-role terminology you see yourself *(revised SPI)*
*   how others see you *(Observer Assessments – 360° feedback)*
*   how the line manager sees a job *(Job Requirements)*

The resulting outputs are designed to meet the needs of three groups:
*   busy executives who have limited time for making important decisions.
*   professional workers whose expertise lies in Training, Management, Development, Management Education and the Human Resource field.
*   those interested in self-management.

Currently INTERPLACE is used by 40% of the UK's top 100 companies and has been translated into a variety of languages for use around the world (Czechoslovakian, Danish, Dutch, Finnish, French, German, Japanese, Norwegian, Slovenian, Spanish and Swedish).

For more information about INTERPLACE and its current development please contact:

BelBin Associates
3-4, Bennell Court
Comberton
Cambridge. UK. CB3 7DS
Tel: +44-(0)1223-264975
Fax: +44-(0)1223-264976
e-mail: info@belbin.com
www.belbin.com

INTERPLACE

BELBIN Team-Role
Expert System

Printed in the United Kingdom
by Lightning Source UK Ltd.
109990UKS00001B/169